MONEY MANAGEMENT FOR TEEN$

16 Lesson$ on "Earning, $aving, Inve$ting, and $pending" and "5 Life Lessons"

Copyright © 2007 by Sheryl Ridley Dorsey
Cover design concept by Kaye Loringer
Photograph courtesy of Reginald Stevenson

All right reserved. This book, or parts thereof may not be reproduced in any form without permission.

Published simultaneously in Canada.

Visit our website at: www.blackstreetinvestmentclub.org

The Library of Congress has catalogued
Sheryl Ridley Dorsey
money management for teens/by Sheryl Ridley Dorsey
ISBN 978-0-9802239-03

Published by TEEN$ & KIDZ

Printed in Canada

MONEY MANAGEMENT FOR TEEN$

16 Lesson$ on "Earning, $aving, Inve$ting, and
$pending" and "5 Life Lessons"

**Sheryl Ridley Dorsey,
C.P.A., M.A.**

Founder of $\mathcal{B}$*lack* $\$$*treet Investment Club* (SM)
(Teen Club)

PEEP INSIDE

"ACHIEVING STANDARDS
OF
EXCELLENCE

FROM THE

CLASSROOM
TO THE
BOARDROOM"©

ACKNOWLEDGEMENTS

First, I would like to thank the members of my teen club, Black $treet Investment Club (B$IC): Romaine Barnes, Ramone Barnes, Jordan Dorsey, Richard Fletcher, Bernard Fowler, Caleb Henry, Collin Hill, Logan Hill, Brandon Johnson, Kenneth Johnson, Ryan Lumpkin, Kurt Phillips, Marcus Phillips, Brandon Rogers, Andrew Stewart, and Sherard Thornhill. I admire their commitment to B$IC and appreciate their contributions to this book. Their profiles may be found at the end of the book.

Special thanks to my family, Thelma Saunders-Noble and Kysha Ridley, and friends, Reginald Stevenson and Pauline Thornhill, for their continuous support and inputs from start to finish of my involvement in this book.

I would like to especially thank Jordan Dorsey, my son and a member of B$IC, for his assistance with the illustrations included in the book.

I wish to thank Ms. Katy Loringer who designed a most suitable concept for the cover of this book and Mr. Kevin Hanley of Burlington County Institute of Technology (and class) for his assistance. Thanks to Nanette Deal White for her review of the first draft and ongoing contributions.

I want to thank Mythili Ravi, my professional editor, for her valuable insights and useful suggestions to improve the quality of this book. I enjoy working with her and looking forward to our next project.

I am thankful to Calvin Claiborne (who's more of a brother) for his incredible patience and understanding; and my friend Pamela Paul-McNeill for her encouraging words.

I am deeply indebted to my mother, Lelia Ridley, for her kindness and generosity and being an immense source of strength.

Thanks to the parents of Black $treet Investment Club for making it possible for their sons to attend the monthly meetings. Special thanks to Alisa Oglesby-Phillips for her involvement, over the years, with the members.

I am forever grateful to Barbara Mealmaker, Former VP of Wachovia Bank, for her generosity; Bernard Narine, Service Director, and the Wachovia Staff for their steadfast support and for granting permission for our investment club to hold our monthly meetings in their boardroom for the past seven years. When I shared with Barbara my concern for lag in financial literacy among our youth, she readily offered the use of Wachovia's boardroom for me to initiate a discussion with a group of enthusiastic boys. I have watched these spirited grow into fine young men over the last seven years. I believe this exposure to a corporate setting and resonance with the purpose of the club have built their confidence and contributed to their growth.

Most importantly, I would like to thank my Savior for placing this vision in my mind to start an investment club for youth, leading to the conception of this book. Through Him, everything is possible!

Hey, how are you? We are from the Black $treet Investment Club (Teen Club). We do some pretty cool stuff here in our investment club for teens. We have put together, in this book, some fun facts and fundas on savings and investment for you guys out there! So, why not grab some snacks out of the "frig", find a comfortable chair, "kick back", and begin reading this book?

Oh, yes, you heard it all right! We said "reading" loud and clear. We know that most of you guys would rather be hanging out with your friends, listening to your iPod, watching DVDs, chatting on your cellphone, or sending e-mails or IMs, than to do some plain, simple "reading". But, mark our words, neither is this an ordinary book nor are we here to bore you or put you to sleep.

We are here to give you some enjoyable and useful reading. For all you know, you might remain in your chair from the first page to the last, while you pick up some tips on how to grow your money. Wow, who would not want that? Oh, by the way, there are also freebies in the form of life lessons.

Happy reading!

Black $treet Investment Club(SM)

(Teen Club)

LESSON 1

Knowledge is Power

"Financial Knowledge = Financial Power"

$\mathcal{D}$id you know that approximately 90% of the decisions you'll make in life will involve money? Consider these questions:

- Which school/college should I attend?
- Should I buy an Apple or a Dell computer?
- Which car should I purchase?
- How much do I contribute to my church or my favorite charitable organization?
- How much should I save and invest?
- Which clothes, music CDs, or video games should I purchase?
- Where and what shall I eat?
- Which is the best place to shop for groceries?
- Which barber/hair salon should I visit?
- To which places can I travel for a vacation?
- Where do I purchase or build my home?
- What kind of insurance should I choose?

As you can see, most crucial life decisions involve money. Yet, our educators have failed to teach students how to manage, save, and invest money. As a result of their oversight, many adults are already neck deep in debt. And, if you are not careful, you may find yourself sinking too.

Do you now realize that money management is an integral part of our everyday life? Are you surprised that our schools do not offer any course to develop money management skills? Are you not puzzled about the lack of knowledge of some adults? Well, you, my friend, have already taken the first step in the right direction by picking up this book.

HOW TO USE THIS BOOK

The book that you are holding is different from your regular textbooks. In a class, you may be expected to read each chapter and answer the questions at the end. Well, consider this book as your cheat sheet to money management. We have followed a Q&A method in developing the content of this book. We have explored the FAQ (frequently asked questions) on money management and have attempted to answer them appropriately. We have used this approach so that you can use your precious time to apply your knowledge.

The next 15 lessons of this book will prepare you to make smart money management decisions. You will also familiarize yourself with common financial pitfalls and learn how to avoid them. There are also five lessons that most of you can relate to and benefit from (in other words, extra credit).

We shall conclude each lesson with a brief workout or exercise. Why? Because, money management is a subject that requires more practice than theory. If you manage to master the fundamentals and complete these workouts, you will gain an enormous confidence to face the financial challenges of the real world.

Okay, guys, sit tight, fasten your seatbelts, and get ready for a thrilling whirlwind ride through the world of money management!

LESSON 2

Allowance

"Getting Paid Based on Results"

Some teenagers receive an allowance from their parents while others do not. For those teenagers who are not currently receiving an allowance, tips will be shared with you on how to convince your parents of the importance of receiving one, and how to arrive at a reasonable amount. And as for those of you who are already receiving an allowance, you could use these same tips to assist you in renegotiating your current allowance with your parents.

What is an allowance?
An allowance is an amount of money given on a regular basis. It is weekly in most cases and bi-weekly in others. Most teens get an allowance as a reward for small errands and chores and there are some teens who receive an allowance "just like that". In other words, they do not have to expend any effort to gain it. Why do some parents choose to give an allowance to their teens and others do not? Many parents give an allowance so that their teens learn how to manage their money. Other parents believe that there are some chores that teenagers must feel responsible to perform, therefore choosing not to give an allowance.

What are these chores? These chores include keeping your room clean, taking your clothes to the laundry room or placing them in the hamper, taking out the trash, sweeping the kitchen floor after dinner, and washing and drying dishes.

Selling the allowance idea to your parents

To successfully sell the allowance idea to your parents, you need to convince them of the benefits of receiving one. Start by explaining to your parents that receiving an allowance can be an educational experience. Emphasize how an allowance will allow you to manage your money, and also teach you to be responsible and value money. In addition, explain to your parents that money is something you'll have to deal with throughout your entire life, and that it is better to make mistakes sooner than later.

How to arrive at an allowance amount

Your allowance amount will depend mainly on your family's financial circumstances. It will also depend on your weekly expenditure, which is the amount of money your parents spend directly on you. To figure out your weekly expenditure, write a list of everything spent on you, on a weekly basis (that is, lunch, church offerings, clothes, movies, notebooks, paper, candy, and music CDs). Total the cost of these expenses. Now, write a list of all of the chores you currently do and any additional chores you feel you can help out with. Assign a reasonable dollar value to each of the chore listed, and total this column. Present both lists to your parents. Discuss the expenses with your parents to decide which of the expenses are your responsibilities and which are those of your parents. Basically, your allowance should equal your responsibilities.

Put it in Writing

Once you negotiate an allowance amount, you may want to draw up a contract to ensure that you hold your end of the deal. The contract should include the names of the parties involved (you and your parents), contract date, responsibilities/chores, allowance amount, and frequency of payment. It should indicate the consequences, should either party break the terms of the contract. Lastly, you may wish to add a paragraph stating the contract is subject to renegotiation, annually. Presto, you've just signed your first contract!

Listen up! If you're successful in convincing your parents to give you an allowance, you should learn how to budget your money so that it lasts the entire week. Remember, in the past, your parents may have paid all of your expenses. Now, if you blow your allowance on purchasing games for your Xbox system, and want to go to the movies with your friends, you may have to wait until the following week. But, if you learn how to budget, you can avoid this trap. See Lesson 14 on Budgeting.

Work Out

Why wait? Now is the perfect time to tour your home and make a list of chores that you can do to earn some extra money.

LESSON 3

Earning Money

"There is No Free Lunch"

*I*n Lesson 2, you learned how to receive an allowance. But, what happens when you want the latest Xbox and your allowance is not enough? What do you do? Well, you can save your allowance for the next two years to buy this system (only to find that the system is outdated), or find a way to earn money to purchase it much sooner. How can you earn money? Try looking around your house for those unidentified chores. Does your garage need to be organized? Does your basement need to be cleaned? Do the closets need to be organized? Whatever it may be, discuss with your parents a fair pay for completing these chores and offer to do them.

In what other ways can you earn money?
How about getting a J-O-B? You could look for a job at fast food restaurants, community pools, movies, amusement parks, summer camps, and shopping malls. In many states, though, you must be at least 14 years old to work. How can you find out about the rules of your state? Check with your school guidance counselor on the required paperwork and the number of hours for which a teenager can work, based on the Child Labor Laws in your residential state.

But, what if you've not yet reached your state's minimum required working age? How can you earn money to buy that Xbox? Why not try working in your neighborhood?

- Wash cars.
- Cut grass.
- Rake leaves.
- Shove snow.
- Run errands.
- Walk your neighbor's dog.
- Coordinate a yard sale.
- Deliver newspapers.
- Sell candy.
- Tutor.
- Baby-sit or pet sit.
- Recycle newspapers and aluminum cans and bottles (you are not only making money but also helping to keep the environment clean).
- Install computer software for adults, who are not familiar with the installation process.
- Design web pages for small businesses and organizations.
- Sell personal items (like clothes and comic books) on E-bay (seek the guidance of your parents).
- Volunteer work – do not rule this out! Volunteer work is a valuable experience. You can learn skills that will enable you to apply for a paying job at a later date. Volunteer work will also come in handy when you seek admission to attend college.

These are just a few jobs that you can do. Now, it is your turn. What ideas do you see?

Important: Never accept a job that will put you in danger, and always discuss any potential job with your parents before acceptance.

Food for Thought
All of the jobs mentioned above can be developed into business opportunities.

Work Out

If you do not meet your state's minimum required working age, look around your home for three chores you can possibly do to earn extra money. Write these chores on a sheet of paper and attach a dollar value to each chore. Next, sit down and negotiate with your parents on these chores and a fair compensation.

But, if you're of working age, look around your community for possible employment opportunities. Write these possibilities on a sheet of paper and discuss them with your parents. With their permission, take action and **"apply"**.

LESSON 4

Savings

"Preparing for Rainy Days"

Saving money in a bank is very important. Why? Because it allows you to park your money in the bank and also earn interest. What is interest? Interest is compensation for the use of your money. In other words, it is the bank's way of thanking you for allowing them to use your money.

For some teens, saving money in a bank is their first encounter with money management. Some parents open a passbook or statement savings account for their children by their eleventh birthday.

What is a passbook/statement account?
A **passbook account** is the booklet you receive from the bank, when you open an account. The way it works is every time you deposit (put in) or withdraw (take out) money, the teller stamps the transaction in your booklet. Your passbook shows these transactions and the amount of interest earned. A **statement account** is similar to a passbook, but it is a print out of your transactions (deposits, withdrawals, fees, and interest earned), during a stated period. This statement is mailed to your home monthly or quarterly. Every teen should have one or the other.

Besides the two aforementioned types of savings accounts, there are others. For example:

- **Certificate of Deposit (CD)**
  Certificate of Deposit is commonly known as CD. Pretty cool! But this is not the same as your music CD. This CD is a piece of paper, an IOU (comes from the literal phonetic spelling of "I Owe You!"), that the bank promises to repay you, the lender, along with some interest. In order to receive the stated amount of interest, you must promise not to touch your money for a specified period. The interest rate for a CD is slightly higher than that for a regular savings account.

  CDs are considered to be a safe and conservative investment, and are insured by the Federal Deposit Insurance Corporation (FDIC). The term "FDIC" will be discussed at the end of this lesson.

- **Money Market Accounts**
  Money market accounts offer many of the benefits of CDs, with the added feature of a checking account, which allows you to write checks and make withdrawals. However, if you exceed the allowed number of checks, the bank will impose a fee. Like CDs, the interest rate is generally higher than that of a regular savings account. Also, like CDs, money market accounts are FDIC insured. **Note:** If you need access to your cash, consider opening a money market account, not a CD.

Why do banks pay a higher interest rate for CDs and money market accounts as compared to basic savings accounts?
The reason is that you allow the banks to "tie-up" your money for a longer period (that is, for 3, 6, 12, 18, or 24 months). In a regular savings account, there is no guarantee that you'll not withdraw all of your money the following morning, thus depriving the bank of access to your money. Another reason is that the minimum that you're required to invest or maintain in your CD or a money market account is higher, than a regular savings account.

Other Savings Accounts

- **Individual Retirement Accounts (IRAs)**
  An IRA is a great way to save taxes and save some money for the future. When you open an IRA, you'll have to decide whether to open a Traditional IRA, a Roth IRA, or an Education IRA. Each has its own rules and tax advantages. The IRA that may be of interest to you is the Education IRA, now called the Coverdell IRA. The Coverdell IRA allows you and your parents to plan for your higher education by saving up to $2,000 every year.

- **Trust Accounts**
  Trust accounts are sometimes established by parents for their children. Parents set up these accounts to ensure that their underage child is financially cared for, should they be unable to do so. These parents allow someone else (trustee, attorney, or executor) to manage their child's money and financial affairs until he/she reaches the stated age (depends upon the state you live in). Like the other savings accounts mentioned, this account grows interest too.

Compounded Interest

As you can see, regardless of which savings account you may choose, and as already mentioned, all of them offer interest, which eventually compounds. But, this is on the assumption that you park your money in the account, without touching it for a specific period. What is compounded interest? Compounded interest is interest paid on your principal, and the interest already accrued (earned) in your account. Compounding interest requires that you do nothing, except "recline" and review your bank statement(s) each month or quarter. This is called "money making money".

Check out how compounding interest works! At age 13, you put $100 into a savings account monthly (that is, CD), with an interest rate of 4% (Table 1). In 10 years, your ending balance will be $14, 983.62.

Table 1: Compounding of Interest for Savings

Age	Year	Ending Balance
13	1	$ 1,248.00
14	2	2,545.92
15	3	3,895.76
16	4	5,299.59
17	5	6,759.57
18	6	8,277.95
19	7	9,857.07
20	8	11,499.35
21	9	13,207.33
22	10	14,983.62

Note: The amount of compounded interest is $2,983.62 over a ten year period ($14,983.62 - $12,000/annual investment)

Source: B$IC

Important: Bank interest rates and fees on savings accounts and savings plans vary. Therefore, you should shop around and select a bank offering the highest rates and lowest fees.

How do banks make money?

If the bank is paying me for the use of my money, how do they stay in business? Banks make money by loaning your money (deposits) to other people for homes, cars, and start-up businesses. Banks will normally charge a higher interest rate to these borrowers. For example, you loan the bank $1,000, through savings, for one year at an interest rate of 2.81%.

The bank then takes your savings of $1,000 and lends it to Jane Doe as a personal loan, and at an interest rate of 9.38% for one year. At the end of the year, you decide to withdraw your money. The bank will repay you $1,000 in principal and $28.10 (interest) for the use of your money.

Meanwhile, the bank receives their $1,000 (principal) and $93.80 (interest) from Jane Doe for the personal loan. Did you notice how the bank just profited from your savings and made $65.70 ($93.80 − $28.10)? The bank calls this the "spread", the difference between the amount loaned and the amount received. This amount may appear to be small, but imagine a bank loaning your parents $300,000-$450,000 for a home mortgage and charging them 9% interest rate over a 30-year period, and then multiply that number by one-half million in loans. Are you getting the point?

Now that you understand how banks make money from the use of your money, let us take a look at how banking history affected your ancestors.

FDIC

Have you heard the "tales" of how some of your ancestors hid their money under the mattress for safekeeping. Have you ever asked yourself "why"? Why would your ancestors leave their monies under their mattress, not earning interest? Well, here is the answer, with some banking history. Many of our ancestors did not believe that their money would be safe with banks. Why? Federal Deposit Insurance Company (FDIC) was created only in 1933 as a result of the Great Depression and the 1929 Stock Market Crash.

What is FDIC? FDIC is operated by the federal government, which guarantees every single penny of your savings up to a sum of $100,000 a bank. However, if the bank goes bankrupt and you have over $100,000 in one bank, you may lose the excess. **Note:** When you begin shopping for a bank, make sure that the bank you use is a member of FDIC.

In closing, know that your money cannot make money by just sitting around and taking up space in your dresser drawer or piggy bank. Nor can your money grow if you are stashing it under the mattress, as many of your ancestors used to do. Let us not repeat history, start saving by banking.

Food for Thought
Did you know that teenagers can invest into an IRA account? Yes. It is true. Teenagers can set up an IRA, and invest up to $2,000 of their earnings.

Work Out

If you do not currently own a regular savings account, speak with your parents about opening one for you. And, when you begin shopping for a bank, make sure that the bank is federally insured (FDIC) and offers competitive interest rates and low fees.

If you do currently own a regular savings account, make sure the institution that you are banking with is federally insured (FDIC) and offers competitive interest rates and low fees. If not, consider switching your savings to another bank.

You can check bank interest rates and fees by visiting www.bankrate.com.

LESSON 5

Checking Accounts

"The Importance of Balance"

*I*t's never too soon for teenagers to learn how to write checks, and eventually open a checking account. Why wait until you attend college or start a family to learn how to do so? That is what some adults did because they did not know better. *But, of course, you now know better.*

What is a checking account? A checking account is a "demand deposit". Meaning, you, as the account owner, can demand or withdraw your money from the bank in the form of a check, transfer of funds, or withdrawal. What is a check? A check is a written order, instructing your bank to transfer money from your account to the check holder.

Is there a "one size fits all" checking account?
No. Banks offer different types of checking accounts.

Types of Checking Accounts

1. **Personal Checking Accounts (without interest):**
   These accounts do not pay interest on the money kept in the bank. Generally, no minimum balance is required. Some banks, though, may charge a fee for processing your checks.

17

2. **Personal Checking Accounts (with interest):** These accounts do pay interest, but you must maintain a minimum balance in your account. If your account balance falls below the minimum, in most cases, your interest will fall too, and the bank may impose or charge a fee.

Note: When you begin shopping for a checking account, locate a bank that offers free checking, and no minimum balance.

Benefits of having a checking account:

1) Convenience: There is no need to search for a branch or an ATM machine to withdraw money.
2) Safety: It does away with the need to carry cash.
3) Recordkeeping: It is a way of tracking your spending.
4) Savings: It is cheaper than money orders and check cashing stores.

Now that you are introduced to two types of personal checking accounts and are aware of the benefits of having one, let us check out the **basic parts of a check.**

Figure 1: Check

(1)		Date_____	(3)	**101** (4)
PAY TO THE				
ORDER OF (2) _____			**$**_____ (5)	
			DOLLARS (6)	
Black Street Bank (7)				
141 Wall Street				
Anywhere, US 10001				
FOR_____ (8)		_____ (9)		
!.33457897(10) 7898598887" (11)		0101" (12)		

1. Name and Address - This information identifies the account holder, which is the same as the owner of the account.
2. Pay to the Order of - This is the person or company that the check is being written to.
3. Date - The date the check was written.
4. Check # - The number of the check that appears on the owner's checkbook.
5. Amount of the Check - This is written in the format of a number.
6. Amount of the Check - This is written out in words and the cents is used as a fraction of 100 cents. To avoid alterations to the check (unauthorized changes), complete the entire line or draw a line to the word "dollars."
7. Name of the Bank - This is the financial institution where you do your checking.
8. Memo - This section is used to write the purpose of the check. For example, to purchase a textbook.
9. Signature - The name on the check (#1) should be the signature on this line.
10. Routing Number - This number identifies the bank for electronic transactions.
11. Checking Account Number – The account that the money will be drawn from.
12. Check Number - This number is the same as the number on the top of the check (#4).

Note: Checks should be written in ink to avoid any altercation.

Check Processing

Now, let us look at how a check works. Your best friend's birthday is six weeks away and you want to buy him/her a special gift – a game for his/her Xbox. (*Wow, everyone needs a friend like you)*. This game is only sold by catalog, and therefore, you need to order the game by mail. After filling out the catalog order form, you must include payment in the form of a check, payable to the catalog company. (**Important:** It is not safe to send cash through the U. S. Postal System). Based on the catalog company's policy, the game will be mailed upon receipt of your order, and after your check has cleared.

If the check you wrote is drawn on the same bank as the catalog company, it clears right away. Checks not drawn on the same account may take 1-2 days. In the past, it has taken some banks 4-7 days to clear checks not drawn on their bank.

When your check reaches the catalog company's bank, the amount of the check is deducted from your account. Approximately two weeks after the end of the month, your bank sends you a statement indicating all of your account's activity during a stated period (usually it is from the first day to the last day of the month). Included with this statement are all the checks you wrote during the month, including the check payable to the catalog company. Banks call these "cancelled checks", meaning that the checks have cleared, or are good for payment. The bank statement and cancelled checks are then used to reconcile your check register.

Reconciling Your Checking Account

What is a Check Register? A check register (Figure 2) is the book that the bank gives you when you open a checking account. The purpose of this book is to record all of your transactions - deposits, withdrawals from ATMs, checks written, bank fees and interest (if applicable). To reconcile, you should cross reference information, such as, the check number and check amount, stated on the bank statement to the check register. If it agrees, a check mark should be indicated in your register, showing that the check has cleared. But, if it does not agree, you must find the difference. Why would there be a difference? Some transactions may not have been recorded in your check register or cleared by the bank. What are these transactions?

- Deposits in Transit (DITs) – DITs are deposits that are recorded in your check register but not cleared by the bank.

- Outstanding (O/S) Checks – O/S checks are checks that are written by you but have not cleared the bank.

- Interests (if applicable) – The amount that is earned on your account, but not recorded in your check register. You may not know the amount of interest until you receive your actual bank statement.

Figure 2:   Check Register

CHECK NO	DATE	DESCRIPTION	TRANSACTION AMOUNT		DEPOSIT AMOUNT		BALANCE 366 97	
231	6-4	Gadgets and More	216	30			216	30
		New cd player					150	67
ATM	6-18	Withdrawl	40	00			40	00
		Spending money					110	67
Ck Crd	6-20	Check card	55	10			55	10
		foodtime groceries					55	57

It is important that you record all transactions in your check register at the time they occur, *not two days later!* If you fail to record your ATM withdrawals or a check that you wrote, you might end up bouncing a check and receiving an NSF notice from the bank.

NSF

What is an NSF? NSF means "not sufficient funds". In other words, you do not have enough money in your account to clear a check that you issued. Since most banks will charge a fee (of about $35) for checks that bounce, it is not recommended that you *"flirt with a zero balance"*. So, how do you avoid this fee? By reconciling (agreeing) your bank statement to your check register, and realizing that both the bank ending balance (statement) and book ending balance (check register) must agree. As already stated, should these two amounts not agree, you must find the difference and immediately record it.

Finally, since banks do not offer "one size fits all" checking accounts, teenagers must do their homework, when shopping for a checking account. **Check out some questions you should ask when opening a checking account.**

- Is there a special account for teens?
- What is the minimum amount to open an account?
- What is the monthly service fee (if applicable)?
- What is the charge for ordering new checks?
- Does the account pay interest? If yes, how much?
- Does the account come with an ATM/Debit card?
- Are there fees associated with using the ATM/Debit card?
- What are the fees for stop payment?

Food for Thought
Learn to reconcile your checkbook to avoid embarrassments, and unnecessary banking fees.

Work Out

With the permission of your parents, write the family bills for one month. After writing the checks, remember to record the date, check number, who the check is written to (payable to), and the check amount in the check register. Next, add the deposits and subtract the checks and other withdrawals (that is, ATM withdrawals). Don't forget to return the checks to your parents for signature and mailing.

The following month, you'll receive the bank statement showing all of the deposits and checks written. If applicable, record the interest and bank fees into the check register. Next, reconcile the check register to the bank statement. *Remember: It must balance!*

LESSON 6

Credit Cards vs. ATM(Debit) Card

"There is a Cost to Using Someone Else's Money"

There are three common types of credit cards or "plastic" cards as these are sometimes called:

1. Visa Card
2. MasterCard
3. Discover

Credit cards generally allow you to purchase goods and services at most stores and businesses.

What is credit? Credit involves an agreement between a financial institution and a buyer. The financial institution agrees to allow a buyer to purchase goods or services from a retailer or a service provider. The buyer leaves with it, and pays for the goods or services at a later date. Generally, the financial institution will not charge any interest for the purchase(s) if the payment is received in full before the due date and within the 20 to 30-day grace period. But, if the buyer does not pay the balance in full and/or pays late, he/she will be "slammed" with interest charges and/or late fees (penalties).

Are you wondering how cool it must be to have a credit card, which allows you to purchase anything you desire? Listen Up! It is not as simple as that. You must be at least 18 years old to apply for a credit card. And, generally, credit card companies require an applicant to complete an application, listing information such as employer's name, yearly income, and other credit information. Credit card companies request this information because they want to make sure the applicant is not a credit risk. A credit risk is a person who may not pay their bills on time, or pay them at all.

However, like everything else, there is an exception to the rule. And, this exception applies to many college students. Check it out!

Credit Cards and College Students

Many times, credit card companies will issue cards to college students who do not have any established credit or income to pay bills. Why do they do so? The reason is that credit card companies are looking to derive income from every possible avenue. According to them, the best customers are those who leave a revolving balance on their account, and many of these customers happen to be college students.

So, how are credit companies being introduced to college students?
Many colleges make financial agreements with credit card companies. Some colleges sell contact information of their students. Some colleges allow representatives of credit card companies to attend events such as homecoming and football games and thus provide access to their students. In return, these colleges may receive monetary rewards. In reality, credit card companies destroy the dreams of many students even before they graduate from college. How?

Soon after receiving their credit cards, many college students begin to use them to purchase "stuff" such as, clothes, music CDs, DVDs, and magazines. Many of their impulse purchases are placed on their credit cards sometimes at an exorbitant interest rate of 23%-30%. Are many college students able to pay for the merchandise they have placed on their card? No! But, needless to say, credit card companies continue to issue cards to college students because they know that they will eventually make payments along with late fees, interests, and penalties.

How do credit card companies collect their money if the college student is refusing or can't pay?
Credit card companies hire collection companies to collect the outstanding balances and late fees. For example, a college student is unable to pay a bill of $1,500. The credit card company employs a collection company, who contacts the student to collect the payment. The student eventually pays the bill, probably four years later, after graduating from college. The student now pays approximately three times the amount that was originally charged (that is, $4,500). You arrive at this number by adding an interest rate of 30% and late charge fees to the purchased amount. And, there is also the service charge for the collection company.

Is the college student now clear and free of worry?
No, because his or her credit has just been damaged as a result of an inability to pay the bill on time. This late payment collection is now on the student's credit report, which will affect his/her future credit ratings. In addition, it may affect the ability of the student to buy something as minor as a cellphone, or as major as a home. This student will likely pay a higher interest rate for future purchases, or even be denied all together. Also, this late payment will become part of the student's FICO score. If you are wondering what a FICO score is, read on!

Fair Isaac Corp. (FICO Score)

There is this geek called "FICO", who runs around with his red pen and pad. His mission is to grade your financial circumstances and show your report card to everyone he meets.

On a serious note, your FICO score defines your credit history. When you do not pay your bills on time, it affects your FICO score, informing lenders that you are a credit risk. Credit scores generally range from 300 to 850 (300 is the worst and 850 is the best). When your score is high, you pay a lower interest rate for purchases. But, when your FICO score is low, you pay a higher interest rate for your purchases. In short, your FICO score determines your financial future.

So, if credit card is a "bad thing", why have one?
Assuming that you are disciplined and pay your bills in full at the end of each month, a credit card can be a "good thing" to have. How? It allows you to build your credit history to eventually purchase a home or car. It helps you to track your expenses, and allows you to maintain a good recordkeeping system. It allows you to consolidate all of your monthly debts. But, most importantly, when you pay your balance in full, and well within the 20 to 30-day grace period, you gain access to free money. *Sadly, many adults fail to understand this simple concept.*

Now let us take a look at the different types of credit card fees, and how they can pile up.

Credit Card Fees

- Finance Charges: This fee can be as high as 30% on the unpaid portion of your credit card bill, each month.
- Annual Fee: Some companies charge a yearly fee for the use of their credit cards. This fee may range from $50 to $100.
- Cash Advance Fee: Avoid this trap. These fees can be steep at 3% to 10% of the advanced cash amount.
- Late Payment Fee: This is another trap. Pay your bill on time to avoid paying banks $35 to $50 in monthly late fees.

Note: Read the fine print on the contract. There may be other hidden fees and penalties.

Here is an example of how finance charges and credit card fees can "pile up". Jane Doe receives a Visa credit card in the mail. Later that day, she goes shopping to purchase a stereo for $500. Jane's finance charge for the use of this card is 20%, and her annual fee is $50. The following month, she forgets to mail her payment to Visa, and the bank charges her $35 in late fees. Jane owes the bank $93 ($50 + $35 + 8/interest), and this is in addition to the payment for the $500 purchase. As you can see, credit card companies are counting on people like Jane to keep them in business. Why? It is because they continue to help their businesses to flourish. So, how do you avoid this trap? You can do so by using an ATM or a Debit card for purchases.

ATM(Debit Card)

Generally, if you have a savings and/or checking account, you probably have an ATM or Debit card. These cards can be used instead of cash. These cards look like credit cards. But they are not credit cards. Unlike a credit card, you do not have a credit line that you can draw from. And, there is no interest charged for purchases.

So, how does an ATM or Debit card work? It moves money for purchases from your checking or savings account to the merchant. It also allows you to withdraw cash or make deposits into your account. This is done by swiping your card in the card reader, entering your PIN (personal identification number) or password and following the prompt to answer a series of questions. When you have completed your transaction, you will get a receipt giving details of your transaction and current balance. Your checking/savings account is automatically adjusted to reflect the amount of the transaction.

Lastly, it is important to know that some banks charge a fee for ATM services. So be sure to check with your bank to find out which banks and ATM machines can be used for free.

Food for Thought
You counteract your investment goals when your debt exceeds your investment. Check it out! Your ROI (return on investment) for Nike's stocks is 11% and your Visa card annual interest rate is 21%. Do you get the point?

Work Out

This exercise is very simple. Do not use credit cards unless you can pay the balance in full, and before the end of each month.

LESSON 7

Bad Debt vs. Good Debt

"Money Should Make Money"

"*A*re you tired of being in debt? Are you tired of having bill collectors calling your home or office? If so, we can show you how to get out of debt in less than one year". Contrary to what the media wants you to believe, all debt is not bad. There are two types of debt – Bad Debt and Good Debt. Bad debt costs you money. Good debt helps make money. Bad debt eats away your earnings. Good debt earns its keep. Bad debt creates a cash outflow. Good debt creates a cash inflow. In other words, bad debt keeps you in poverty, while good debt helps create wealth. Sounds simple! So, what is the problem? The problem is that many adults are converting good debt into bad debt. How? Read on.

Bad Debt

Debt turns into bad debt when borrowers choose to misuse their debt privilege. When creditors extend credit or loans, they allow borrowers the privilege of using their money at a cost. Sometimes, people tend to abuse this privilege by not paying their debt on time, or not paying at all. One of the most abused debt privileges in America is credit card debt. Millions of Americans are in debt due to two words -- "Charge it"!

31

Many people are using credit cards to purchase depreciable assets. Depreciable assets are defined as assets that lose their value, over a period of time. An example of a depreciable asset is your sneakers. Have you noticed that when your parents charge, on their credit card, your sneakers for $120-$150, two to four weeks later the heels begin to run down, if you have not outgrown them first? The sneakers no longer have that "fresh look". Those sneakers have lost their value. And, to top it off, the sneakers may not be paid for, if only the minimum payment is being paid to the credit card company.

Good Debt

Let us now look at good debt. Good debt helps improve your life over a longer period. It also helps create financial wealth. **Below are four examples of good debt, and how sometimes good debt becomes bad debt.**

1. Mortgage Debt
2. Student Loan Debt
3. Car Loan Debt
4. Rental Property Debt (OPM Debt)

1. Mortgage Debt

A mortgage is considered to be good debt and a great investment. Why? It allows your parents to purchase a home. When your parents eventually sell their home, its value will generally have gone up, allowing them to profit from its sale. Mortgage debt becomes bad debt when parents purchase "Joneses" homes rather than affordable homes. What are Joneses homes? Joneses homes are homes that people cannot afford but buy anyway. Their goal is to "keep up with the Joneses" (neighbors) at any cost. What are affordable homes? Affordable homes are homes that allow people to make mortgage payments on time, pay their other essential bills, and have money set aside to save and invest.

2. **Student Loan Debt**

A student loan is also considered to be good debt because it allows you to invest in your future. The problem is that parents and teenagers are planning much later rather than earlier for college. Planning for college should occur when you enter into your first classroom door, not the college door. But, because many families fail to do so, many college students are graduating with "huge" college loans (to the extent of $20,000-50,000).

While it is difficult for many to attend college without using student loans, planning for college is a must. Your parents must plan for your education. But, you too need to take responsibility for setting some money aside. This is the only way you may avoid those "huge" college loan payments that many students and parents are responsible for repaying after graduation.

Note: Statistics show that college graduates make 62% more money than high school graduates.

3. **Car Loan Debt**

Car loan debt is also a good and acceptable debt. However, it is only acceptable if you need a car and can afford the payments. A car becomes bad debt when you purchase something that you cannot afford. Meaning, if you are strapped for money, you should not try to purchase a latest model sports car. You should consider purchasing something that is more affordable.

As a FYI, cars are considered to be an acceptable debt, but are also known as depreciable assets. Why?

Because a car begins to lose its value the moment it is driven off the lot. So, why is it considered to be a good and acceptable debt? In most cases, a car is a necessity, allowing you to work and earn money.

4. **Rental Property Debt (O.P.M. Debt)**

Rental property debt is what we call "OPM." debt (other people's money). You have OPM debt when you borrow someone else's money (here, the bank) for investment purposes. A great example of the use of OPM is real estate. When you borrow money to buy rental property for investment purposes, you receive rental income. What is rental income? Rental income is what tenants pay you for living in your property. The way it works is that you charge your tenant enough money to cover your expenses. The expenses include monthly mortgage payment, insurance, taxes, repairs and maintenance in addition to an excess to cover your profit. You then take the profit and reinvest it into the rental property (improvements) or buy other properties. *Oh, by the way, this is how Donald Trump made his billions.*

So, how can OPM debt become bad debt? This debt is not likely to be converted into bad debt unless it is no longer a positive cash flow, in other words, you may spend more than what you collect from your tenants. And, you are unable to sell the property.

As you can see, all debt is not equal. So, the next time you hear that radio advertisement "Are you tired of being in debt?", think to yourself, only if that debt is losing value over time. The goal is to use good debt when it is appropriate, and avoid bad debt as much as possible. Good debt will always improve your life over a period of time.

Food for Thought
Open your mind to new possibilities.

Work Out

Spend some time with your friends and family discussing the importance of not being slave to bad debt.

LESSON 8

The "Pie Chart" Rule

"The Importance of Discipline"

*W*hat is the "Pie Chart" rule ? The "Pie Chart" rule simply explains how to spend money that you have earned and received (allowance and gifts). Below is a diagram (Figure 3) of the "Pie Chart", and a brief explanation of its application.

Figure 3: Pie Chart Rule on Money Management

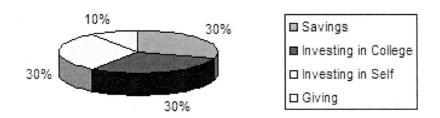

Source: B$IC

The "Pie Chart" rule divides the pie into four slices:

- 30% is sliced for savings (like certificates of deposits).
- 30% is sliced for investing into your college education (that is, stocks or mutual funds).
- 30% is sliced for investing into yourself. This is the money that you can use to start your own business, buy

the latest music CD, concert tickets, or video games.
- 10% is set aside for giving (like a church offering).

Note: You will learn more about investing in the forthcoming lessons.

Why do you need rules for spending?
Without rules, most, if not all of your money would become part of the last slice of the pie (that is, music CDs and video games), "investing into yourself." This becomes a major problem when it is time to attend college and you have not set aside money for college expenses, such as books. How do you avoid this trap? You can do so by remembering to use the "Pie Chart" rule for spending.

Note: Once you begin paying your own rent, buying groceries, paying a car loan, and other expenses, you need to re-evaluate the slices and divide your pie differently. The slices will change in size and type. For example, the slice, "invest into yourself," will change to "pay yourself first." Meaning, always take at least 10% off the top to use for savings and investments. This is what many adults forget to do, which leads them to have meager savings and investments.

Work Out

Make a list of all the money you receive weekly or monthly (earned income, allowance, and gifts). Indicate the dollar amount next to the description. After indicating the dollar amount, total it and draw a pie chart (indicating the 30/30/30/10 rule). State how much of your money will be sliced for each pie. For example, if you receive a weekly allowance of $20, multiply the percentage of each rule by $20 and write the answer in the appropriate slice. Now, implement the plan.

LESSON 9

Different Types of Income

"Windows to Wealth"

$\mathcal{D}$o you believe that earned income, income you work for, is the only type of income? If you answered no, you are correct. There are three basic types of income:

1. **Earned Income:** This comes from a job and is in the form of a paycheck. When you ask your parents to buy you an iPod, their response may be, "you need to get a JOB". They are actually telling you to work and earn your money.

2. **Portfolio Income:** This comes from investments such as stocks, bonds, and mutual funds. These investments allow your money to work even while you are asleep. **Note:** You will learn more about portfolio income in the forthcoming lessons.

3. **Passive Income:** This comes from real estate. This does not refer to the house that you and your family may be living in. This income comes from rental property that your family may own and rent to tenants.

   Passive income also comes from royalties from copyrights and patents/licensing. Royalty income comes from songs or writing books or developing software. It is income that entertainers such as Beyonce, P Diddy, Eminem (Slim Shady), J Lo, Tye Tribett, and J K Rowling receive from CDs, DVDs, and books that you purchase. Also, the albums of legends like Bob Marley and Elvis Presley continue to generate royalty income long after their death.

Let us not forget Bill Gates, who followed through with his idea and came out with his Microsoft patent. His personal net worth is about $57 billion in 2007.

More on Earned Income

Earned income is income that provides dependency. What does this mean? Earned income is income that you work at a "J-O-B" to obtain. In exchange for your services, you receive a paycheck from your employer on a regular basis. Thus, you are depending on your employer for this earned income.

Earned income is also referred to as "three-fourths income". What is the reason for such a name? It is because a portion of your earned income goes to "Uncle Sam" (IRS) and his sons (state and/or local tax agencies). By the time you receive your share of your hard-working money, you find yourself bringing home just a little more than three-fourths of each dollar. Ouch!!!!!

So, how do you maximize your earned income, after Uncle Sam and his sons have grabbed a share of your hard earned money? You can do so by creating portfolio and passive income with your three-fourths income.

Work Out

Discuss with your parents the various sources of income that they have accumulated over the years.

LESSON 10

Stocks

"If You are Going to Buy It, Why Not Own a Piece of It"

*I*t is never too early to begin thinking about investing in stocks. You don't have to be wealthy to buy stocks. As a teenager, you can invest a small amount to begin meeting your long-term financial goals.

What are stocks? Stocks represent ownership of a company, through an investment, with the expectation of receiving a return on your investment (ROI). If you own a company's stock, you are a shareholder or stockholder of the company. But, before you consider investing, you need to do your homework. You need to understand the fundamentals of stocks, raise questions, and research the company to find the right answers.

WHAT YOU SHOULD KNOW ABOUT STOCKS:

- Generally, stocks become available, when a private company needs money to expand their services or products. To do so, **private companies** "go public". By **"going public"**, a company decides to sell shares of their stocks in exchange for money. These shares are sold to people of all walks of life (companies, partnerships, as well as individuals). The owners of the company are now officers, reporting to the stockholders or investors.

- The **"initial public offering" (IPO)** is the first time that a company's stocks are sold to the public. Investment banking firms handle IPO transactions. They are responsible for purchasing all of the stocks, setting the stock prices, and finding investors, who are willing to buy the IPO stocks.

- Ownership of stocks in a company is represented by a **stock certificate**. Since many public companies track ownership electronically, you may not receive an actual paper stock certificate. Instead, many companies issue computerized transaction statements to their stockholders, showing their ownership.

- Each stockholder is entitled to **vote at an annual meeting** to elect the directors of a company. Most of the time, stockholders with a small fraction of stocks and those who are unable to attend the meetings, vote by proxy. **Proxy** means to submit your vote by mail rather than in person. However, if you own a considerable amount of stocks with a company, you may want to attend its annual meeting.

- Companies that make profits pay out **dividends** (returns for use of money) to their stockholders. Such companies call these stocks "income stocks". **Income stocks** allow you to receive a steady income from your investment, assuming that the company makes a profit.

- Some companies may use their profits to make further improvements in their business rather than pay divi-dends, or may prefer to pay small dividends. These stocks are called "growth stocks". **Growth stocks** are expected to grow in value because their companies have reinvested to improve or expand their products or services, and may go on to make more money for their stockholders.

- At the end of the year, public companies present **annual reports** to their stockholders. The annual report gives a snapshot of the company's performance in the reported year. This report also describes the company's future plans.

- Unlike the way some teenagers trade baseball cards, stocks are traded daily. Stocks are traded on exchanges such as the **New York Stock Exchange (NYSE)** and the **American Stock Exchange (AMEX)**. Exchanges are special places where stocks are bought and sold. NYSE and AMEX are the primary exchanges in the United States.

- A person who **trades** (buys and sells) stocks for a client is called a **broker**. Generally, you pay a broker for such trading services.

Questions you should asked yourself before buying stocks

Do you find the idea of buying stocks in a company exciting? If yes, you may be able to make a lot of money. What if the company you invest in fails and you lose some or all of your money? Would you be upset? If the answer is yes, consider purchasing a mutual fund. Stockholders may make money or lose money by investing into the stock market. There is no guarantee that you won't "lose your shirt". Therefore, it is important to do your homework and only invest the money that you put aside for investment.

What are my goals?
If your goal is to buy the latest Xbox, music CDs, and clothes, investing is not the way to go. If you want to frequently withdraw your money, investing is not for you. Consider purchasing a three-six month CD (certificate of deposits) from your bank. Investing into stocks requires that you "tie up" your money. Overnight successes are rare! It could be at least four years or more before you can expect to see a real return on your investment, or make money.

How do you determine which stocks to buy?
Selecting the most profitable stock is not the only way to invest. You can invest based on your beliefs, interests, or knowledge. You can also invest in a company based on your faith in the quality of its products or services. Here are some examples of companies that have gone public (on the stock exchange):

- Nike
- AOL
- Microsoft
- Dell Computers
- Apple
- McDonald's
- Coca Cola
- Pepsi
- Wal-Mart
- ExxonMobil
- Adidas

What is a "Bull"/ "Bear"?
A **"bull"** is a person who is optimistic or bullish about the future of the stock market or a specific company. A bull believes that the stock prices will go up. A **"bear"** is someone who is less enthusiastic about the future of the stock market or the value of a particular company. A bear has no confidence in

44

the stock market. If you are a bear, you should not be trying to hang out with the bulls.

What does it mean to "Buy Low and Sell High"?

Generally, buy low and sell high means to buy the stock at the lowest price possible and sell at the highest price possible. This is how you will make your money.

What is SEC?

The **Security Exchange Commission** (SEC) regulates the securities industry (stock market) as a whole. Its primary purpose is to protect investors against fraudulent and manipulative practice in the securities market. In other words, it polices the security market, ensuring fairness and honesty. SEC also ensures that companies adequately disclose their financial position to the public.

What is a stock index and who are the "players"?

A **stock index** is a group of stocks, whose selection is based on certain criteria. There are three major "players" who dominate the stock field and are responsible for telling you "what's up or what's down" in the stock market.

1. **The Dow Jones Industrial Average (DJIA)** – The Dow is an index made up of 30 blue chip companies. A blue chip generally refers to the stock of a large, solid and reputable company. A blue chip company is considered to be a safer investment because of its low risk. Here are some of the 30 stocks that are included in the Dow:

    o   AT&T (T)
    o   Coca-Cola (KO)
    o   Disney (DIS)

o   Exxon Mobil (XOM)
o   Home Depot (HD)
o   IBM (IBM)
o   McDonald's (MCD)
o   Microsoft (MSFT)
o   Wal-mart (WMT)

Note: The symbols will be explained toward the end of this lesson.

2. Standard & Poor's 500 (S&P 500)
No, this is not the car race show you watch on your television. S&P 500 is a basket of 500 stocks, unlike the Dow, which includes only 30 stocks. Most of the stocks reported in the Dow are also included in S&P 500. Some people feel that this index is more reliable than the Dow because S&P 500 tracks much more of the entire stock market.

3. NASDAQ Composite Index
NASDAQ Composite Index is made up of thousands of stocks traded on the NASDAQ exchange.

What is the NASDAQ exchange?
NASDAQ (acronym of National Association of Securities Dealers Automated Quotations) stocks are listed and traded electronically, rather than on the floor, like the NYSE and the AMEX.

How do I determine how much of a company I own?
The ownership of a company you invested in is calculated by the percentage of stocks outstanding, and the number of shares that you purchased. For example, the company has 20,000 shares (stocks) outstanding. You own 2,000 shares (stocks),

which is the equivalent of 10%. In other words, you have 10% ownership in the company.

Are stocks risky?

Buying stocks can be risky because the prices of stocks fluctuate daily. If the company goes bankrupt (out of business), you can lose your entire investment. If the company soars (profits), you can benefit. Remember that investing is all about taking risks in the hope of receiving a return on your investment.

What is a Return on Investment (ROI)?

A ROI is the percentage that you have earned or lost as a result of your investment. There are two types of returns -- positive and negative. A positive return on your investment means that you have made money. A negative return on your investment means that you have lost money.

What are some of the factors that contribute to my tolerance for risk?

1. Age
2. Financial needs, such as college expenses.
3. Level of debt
4. Investment objective(s)
5. Health

As a teenager, the age factor is on your side. Unlike your parents and grandparents, you can tolerate the mood changes of the market (ups and downs). *Who said being young doesn't have any advantage?*

Why do stock prices of companies rise?

1. More people are buying and less people are selling.
2. New executives are hired to manage the company.
3. The company has and/or is expecting an exciting new product or service.
4. The company lands a big contract.
5. Rumors
6. The company announces that another company is buying it at a higher price.
7. The industry and/or the market is heated up.
8. Other stocks in the industry too go up.
9. No rhyme or reason

Why do stock prices of companies fall?

1. More people are selling and less people are buying.
2. A top executive leaves the company.
3. Crime/Fraud committed by senior management.
4. Profit and/or sales are slipping.
5. The company loses a major contract.
6. Another company introduces a better product.
7. International competition
8. Rumors
9. The industry has cooled down.
10. War/Terrorism
11. The country is in recession.
12. No rhyme or reason

How can I achieve the best possible return while reducing some of my risks?

-   Know when to sell. Think about how long you will be investing. If the stocks go up by 30%-40%, will you sell? If the grass is greener on the other side, will you sell? *You must have an exit strategy!*

- Determine the level of risk you are willing to take. If the stock goes down by 10%, will you sell? *Know when to dump your stocks before your losses get out of hand!*

- Pick a diversified basket of stocks (mixture of industries).

- Select investments that will help you achieve your goal (for example, aggressive stocks vs. conservative stocks).

Finally, how do I buy stocks?

- You can buy stocks directly from the company. This is known as the DRIP Plan. *No, not the water from a faucet.* DRIP is short for **Dividend Reinvestment Investment Plan (DRIP).** DRIP is a plan that offers you a simple and less expensive way of purchasing stocks directly through the company. It allows you to reinvest your dividends, and buy additional stocks. Why else should you use DRIP? You should use DRIP to save broker fees. Also, some companies that participate in DRIP allow you to purchase stocks for as little as $250. To find out whether a company participates in DRIP, visit its website or call the company directly.

- You can use a broker. If you decide to use a broker, be sure to ask and understand all of the fees associated with their services.

Stock Table

Now, let's learn how to read a New York Stock Exchange table:

Table 2: NYSE Table

52W high	52W low	Stock	Ticker	Div	Yield %	P/E	Vol 00s	High	Low	Close	Net chg
s45.39	19.75	ResMed	RMD			52.5	3831	42.00	39.51	41.50	-1.90
11.63	3.55	Revlon A	REV				162	6.09	5.90	6.09	+0.12
77.25	55.13	RioTinto	RTP	2.30	3.2		168	72.75	71.84	72.74	+0.03
31.31	16.63	RitchieBr	RBA			20.9	15	24.49	24.29	24.49	-0.01
8.44	1.75	RiteAid	RAD				31028	4.50	4.20	4.31	+0.21
s38.63	18.81	RobtHalf	RHI			26.5	6517	27.15	26.50	26.50	+0.14
51.25	27.69	Rockwell	ROK	1.02	2.1	14.5	6412	47.99	47.00	47.54	+0.24

Column 1 Column 2 Column 3 Column 4 Column 5 Column 6 Column 7 Column 8 Column 9 Column 10 Column 11 Column 12

Col 1-2	52 Weeks is a year. The Hi and Lo are the highest and lowest prices the stocks have been traded for over the past year. The numbers may be given in fractions, 1/8 = 12 ½ cents and 5/8 = 62 ½ cents.
Col 3	The Stock is the company name. It may be abbreviated to save space.
Col 4	Sym is the "ticker" symbol that represents the company. For example, Rite Aid Company is RAD.
Col 5-6	This is the cash you expect to receive from your investment in a particular stock. Div is the estimated dividend to be paid per share. The % is what percentage of your investment you'll receive in dividends. Yld stand for "yield".
Col 7	PE stands for "price-earnings ratio." It refers to the relations between the price of one share, and the per share annual earning of the company.
Col 8	Vol 00s is how many share of stock were traded that day. Take the figure listed and multiply by 100. Stock is usually sold in "lots" of 100 called a "round lot." Less than 100 shares is called an odd lot.
Col 9	Hi is the highest price for the day.

Col 10   Lo is the lowest price for the day.

Col 11   Close is the price of the share in its last trade of the day.

Col 12   Net Chg is the comparison of the price at the close of the day with the price at the close of the previous day's trading. If the price went down, it is shown by a minus sign (-). If the price went up, it is shown be a plus sign (+).

Source: www.investopedia.com

Whew! You have just covered hoards of information. You should be extremely proud of yourself. Are you now feeling "bullish?" If you are, why not set aside some time to research a company of interest. If you wish to invest in the company after a thorough research, consult your parents, and possibly a broker, about your investment interest.

Food for Thought
Consider investing your money, instead of spending it on "stuff".

Work Out

Pick two of your favorite companies and begin tracking their performance on a weekly basis. You can do so by reading the Wall Street Journal, or watching a business television channel like Bloomberg that monitors stock performances, or check online at www.amex.com.

LESSON 11

Mutual Funds

"Don't Put all of your Eggs In One Basket"

*W*hat is a Mutual Fund? A mutual fund consists of a group of people pooling their money to own a portfolio of investments, such as stocks, bonds, or money markets. Unlike stocks, a mutual fund allows you to mutually own many companies through the purchase of one fund.

In the previous lesson, it was explained how investing in stocks requires your time and effort to ensure that your stocks are performing well. But, mutual funds require just the opposite. Mutual funds are for people who neither have the time to frequently review their accounts online, nor the time to browse through the Wall Street Journal on a daily basis. But they, too, have the desire to grow their money with some diversification.

What is diversification?
Diversification simply means that funds are invested in a variety of markets or a mixture of investments (such as stocks, bonds, money markets, real estate, and CDs). The diversification can be based on different industries or the same industry. Why would you want diversification? You want diversification to reduce your risks. If one investment is not performing well, you may have other investments in that same account that are performing well, giving you a chance to

53

earn a return on your investment, or at a minimum, breakeven. For example, if you own a Managed Allocation Mutual Fund (mixture of equity and bonds), and stocks are down, but the bonds are up (due to the interest rates), you may incur a return on your investment, or experience a breakeven (no gain and no loss). In other words, the "ups" of your bonds may offset the "downs" of your stocks.

Different Types of Mutual Funds

In the above example, we used Managed Allocation Mutual Fund to describe how a mutual fund works. But, there are many other types of mutual funds too.

- Stocks Funds (Equity Funds) allow you to own stocks with different companies.

- Bonds Funds allow you to own different types of bonds or own one bond (municipal bonds, US government bonds, and/or corporate bonds).

- Money Market Funds allow you to own short-term investments such as certificate of deposits. It is also a safe place to store your money for emergency use.

- Balanced Funds allow you to own both stocks and bonds.

- Real Estate Investment Trust Funds (REIT) allow you to own real estate (that is, commercial property or apartment buildings).

Advantages of Mutual Funds

- Diversification is one of the main advantages of a mutual fund. As already mentioned, if a fund has an investment that is doing well, it may offset another investment that is not doing so well. Remember that you are hoping for more "ups" than "downs".

- Another advantage is that some mutual funds allow you to make a minimum investment amount. For instance, you may only need $250 to purchase a mutual fund, whereas, with some stocks, you may need to buy a set number of shares or purchase a minimum amount of $2,500.

- Your funds are operated by professional money managers.

Disadvantage of Mutual Funds

- The disadvantage of a mutual fund is that the return on this investment is usually less than the return on stocks. But it also has lower risk than stocks.

Fund Managers

Fund managers are responsible for managing your fund(s). Their responsibility includes researching and selecting different securities for funds. **Important:** When seeking a fund manager, be sure to check their track records to confirm their success rates in managing mutual fund accounts. Mutual funds can look good on paper. But if you don't do your homework, the fees can rob you of your gain. Check out the example!

You purchase a $6,000 mutual fund and receive an annual average return of 10%. Your fund manager's fees are 2%. Guess what? Your annual average return is not 10%, but 8% (10% - 2%). Another way of saying this is that your fund manager receives 20% (10% x .02) of your annual return.

Types of Fees Involved in Setting up a Mutual Fund

1. Management Fees – fees to administer the account
2. Load Fees – fees for investing your funds
    a. Front-end Load fees: Investors pay these fees when they purchase their shares.
    b. Back-end Load Fees: Investors pay these fees when they redeem their shares.
    c. No-Load Fees: Fees are involved, but investors are not required to pay commission.

Generally, the fees charged to administer a mutual fund account are listed in the prospectus.

Prospectus

Just like stockholders, mutual fund investors also receive a prospectus. What is a prospectus? A prospectus is a written statement describing the fund's objectives (what it hopes to do) and its current and past performance. This report explains the minimum investment amount, the fees, and the level of risk. A level of risk is how much risk you're willing to allow your money to be susceptible to a loss.

Mutual Fund Table

Table 3: Mutual Fund Table

52W high	52W low	Fund	Spec.	Fri. NAVPS Schg	%chg	——Wkly NAVPS—— high	low	cls	$chg	%chg
Montrusco Bolton Funds										
11.71	10.12	Bal Plus	*N	-0.08	-0.76	10.58	10.50	10.50	0.02	0.15
12.50	10.25	Growth Plus	*N	-0.10	-0.96	10.89	10.78	10.78	0.02	0.22
31.39	24.78	Quebec Growth	*FR	0.05	0.17	26.97	26.75	26.97	0.43	1.61
13.78	7.24	RSP Intl Growth	*N	-0.08	-1.01	7.45	7.36	7.36	-0.03	-0.41
11.16	9.09	Value Plus	*N	-0.07	-0.75	9.39	9.32	9.32	0.01	0.14
9.65	8.90	World Inc	*N	-0.04	-0.40	9.52	9.39	9.48	0.04	0.43
Montrusco Select Funds CS(n)										
12.87	10.49	Balanced	*N	-0.04	-0.37	10.85	10.80	10.81	0.05	0.45
16.32	12.11	Balanced +	*N	-0.05	-0.43	12.57	12.52	12.52	0.06	0.45
10.16	9.86	Bond Index +	X*N	-0.03	-0.32	10.35	10.30	10.30	0.04	0.37

Column 1   Column 2   Column 3   Column 4   Column 5   Column 6   Column 7   Column 8   Column 9   Column 10   Column 11

As with the stock market, mutual funds are listed in the financial pages of newspapers. Here's how you read a Mutual Fund Table (Table 3):

Col 1 & 2   52-Week High and Low – These show the highest and lowest prices the mutual fund has experienced over the previous 52 weeks (one year). This typically does not include the previous day's price.

Col. 3   Fund Name – This column lists the name of the mutual fund. The company that manages the fund is written above in bold type.

Col. 4   Fund Specifics – Different letters and symbols have various meanings. For example, "N" means no load, "F" is front end load, and "B" means the fund has both front and back-end fees.

Col. 5   Dollar Change – This states the dollar change in the price of the mutual fund from the previous day's trading.

Col. 6   % Change – This states the percentage change in the price of the mutual fund from the previous day's trading.

Col. 7   Week High – This is the highest price the fund traded at during the past week.

Col. 8   Week Low – This is the lowest price the fund traded at during the past week.

Col. 9   Close – The last price at which the fund was traded is shown in this column.

Col. 10   Week's Dollar Change – This represents the dollar change in the price of the mutual fund from the previous week.

Col. 11   Week's % Change – This shows the percentage change in the price of the mutual fund from the previous week.

Source: www.investopedia.com

As you read, mutual funds have pros and cons. Therefore, you must do your homework. Familiarize yourself with the different types of funds, understand your risk, and the fees involved in purchasing a mutual fund.

Food for Thought
Shop for a fund manager who has a successful track record and charges a reasonable fee.

Work Out

If Mutual Funds are for you, spend more time learning about the different funds available. Check out www.mutualfunds.about.com.

LESSON 12

Bonds

"Making the Grade"

$\mathcal{W}$hat are bonds? Bonds are essentially a form of a contract for debt that is sold to the public. In other words, a bond is an IOU issued by a borrower to a lender. How do bonds come about? Bonds come about when companies, municipalities, or the government have huge financial requirements like building offices or schools or paying salaries. The borrowers go out to the public to borrow money to fund these costs. The borrower (company, municipality, or the government) agrees, in writing, to repay the lender.

Take a look at some of the elements written into a bond contract:

- loan amount (principal)
- agreed-upon interest rate (sometimes called "coupon rate")
- how often interest will be paid
- maturity date

Bonds are known as a fixed income (steady income) investment. You, as the lender, know how much interest you will receive in return for your investment. This interest is usually paid semi-annually, and generally does not vary.

Since bonds are considered to be a conservative or safe investment, they are not as attractive as stocks. However, unlike stocks, the performance of bonds is usually irrelevant. A bond investor will likely receive interest on a loan on the due date and the principal on its maturity date, regardless of the performance of the bonds. This is one of the advantages of investing into bonds. Another advantage is that bonds may keep you afloat when your other investments (such as stocks) are going through troubled time.

But, just as there are advantages, there are also disadvantages:

- You may lose part of your principal if you sell before the maturity date.

- You can lose part or all of your principal if the issuer defaults on the loan, (unable to repay the loan)

So, how do you limit your exposure to defaults? To limit your exposure to defaults, you should choose high quality bonds when investing. Bonds are graded or "rated" by agencies such as Standard and Poor's (S&P) and Moody's Investor Services. These rating agencies consider the financial health of the issuers before assigning them suitable grades. The purpose of the bond rating is to show the stability of a company. The grade also shows how likely the issuer may default or fail to repay the loan. The higher the grade, the higher is the quality of bonds. Junk bonds are the lowest rated bond. For example, an "AAA" or "Aaa" (*not to be confused with the auto club*) is the highest grade that an issuer can receive. Anything below a "B" is considered to be a junk bond (unacceptable). *Aren't we glad Moody and Standard are not responsible for grading our exams?*

Listed below are different types of bonds and a description of each:

- **Corporate Bonds** normally carry a higher interest rate than government bonds. The reason is that there is a potential for the company to go bankrupt and default on the loan.

- **Callable Bonds** grant the borrower the right to pay off the bonds earlier than the maturity date.

- **Government Bonds** (like treasury bills and treasury bonds) do not pay state and local taxes on the interest you earn and receive.

- **State and Municipal Bonds** (called **munis**) are popular and have tax free advantages too. Unlike other investments, these are the bonds that Uncle Sam (federal government) is unable to bite into. And, generally, if you live in the state where the bond is issued, you are exempted from state and local taxes too.

- **High Yield Bonds** known as **junk bonds** are considered to be bonds of high risk. These are corporate bonds that did not make the grade.

Like stocks, bonds can be purchased from a broker. Bonds are generally sold in denominations of $1,000. One of the best and easiest ways to own bonds is through the purchase of a mutual fund. As stated earlier, mutual funds offer diversification, allowing you to "mix-up" your investments, with different types of bonds from different issuers, reducing your exposure to risk.

Are you overwhelmed? If so, let us simplify this lesson with an example. Assume that you invest into a $1,000 (face value) bond with the City of New York. You submit a check to the agency and receive a contract stating the term (10 years) and interest rate (current yield) of 7%. At a stated period during the year, you will receive $70. If the interest income is paid semiannually, you will receive $35 twice a year. Finally, at the end of 10 years, you will receive your principal of $1,000. It is that simple.

7%/$1,000 = $70 annually
or
$35 semi-annually

Note: Because bond commissions vary, it won't hurt to do your homework first. Shop around.

Work Out

If you are interested in bonds, why don't you spend time to understand it better? Check out www.investinginbonds.com.

LESSON 13

Taxes

"Uncle Sam and His Sons"

𝒴ou have finally decided to take the advice of your parents. You have found a J-O-B! You can now stop asking your parents for money, because you are bringing home a "phat" check. But, wait, you have just had a "rude awakening". This so-called "phat" check is not so "phat" after all. You are wondering what happened to your check. *Congratulations!* You have just been informally introduced to Uncle Sam and his sons, through means of earned income, which triggered taxes.

Earned income includes wages, salaries, tips, and net earnings from self-employment. Generally, if you are receiving earned income, you must pay payroll taxes. The way it works is Uncle Sam (IRS) and his sons (state and local government) take their money from your gross income before you can get your hands on it. Uncle Sam and his sons call this "withholding taxes". You, however, get a chance to take home the "leftovers" (net pay). This is the amount of money that you will need to figure out how to spend wisely.

What are taxes?
Taxes refer to the amount of money that your federal, state, and/or local government takes out of your check. Why does the government take taxes out of your hard earned money?

The reason the government takes taxes out of your check is to pay for the goods and services that are being provided to you and your family. What type of services does the government provide? The government provides garbage collection services, street cleaning, street lights, law enforcement, military, library, fire stations, and so on. The government helps to support hospitals, colleges, public schools, and care for the elderly and poor. The government also subsidizes school lunches and conducts food inspections.

How much tax will Uncle Sam and his sons take?
This will depend on how much money you make. Generally, the higher your taxable income, the more taxes you will pay to Uncle Sam and his sons.

What are the different types of taxes withheld from an employee paycheck?

a. Federal Withholdings are taxes paid to the federal government for services, such as armed forces and the elderly.

b. State Withholdings are taxes paid for state services provided to you and your family, such as education.

c. FICA Withholdings (Social Security and Medicare) are taxes paid for the Social Security Program and provision of medical insurance for the elderly and disabled.

d. UI/DI Withholdings (Unemployment and Disability) are taxes that may or may not be applicable in your state. If applicable, the purpose of these withholdings is to set aside income in case of a temporary unemployment or inability to work due to illness.

e. Local Withholding are taxes paid for city/township services provided to you and your family.

Determining your Payroll Taxes/Reporting

Now that you know why you pay taxes and where your tax money goes, let's look at how your payroll taxes are determined and reported. Generally, before you begin working, you meet with the human resource/personnel department to complete a form called **W-4 (Wage 4)**. The W-4 is the form that determines how much tax your employer will withhold from each paycheck. This form requires that you print your personal information such as name, address, and social security number on the form. This form also requires that you answer questions regarding the number of exemptions you are claiming. Each exemption reduces the amount of taxes withheld from your paycheck. As a teenager, you are considered one exemption and your tax status is assumed to be "single".

> **Caution:** Do not consider fibbing on your W-4. If so, it will catch up with you when you file your tax returns. And, you'll find that you owe loads of money to Uncle Sam and his sons.

With each paycheck, there is a statement attached. This statement is called an **earning statement**. The earning statement tells you the number of hours you have worked, your hourly rate, how much you earned during a stated period, and the amount of payroll taxes and other authorized deductions withheld from your paycheck. It gives you year-to-date (YTD) information for your wages, taxes and deductions. In addition, it has your personal information like name, address, and social security number.

At the end of the year, you will receive a **Wage and Tax Statement called W-2** from your employer. A W-2 (Figure 4) is a statement that shows all of the wages that you received, and the taxes withheld, during the year. Each employee receives his or her W-2 at the beginning of each year (on or before January 31st) for the previous year. For each employer you work for in the year, you'll receive a W-2 to be filed with your federal, state, and/or local tax returns. In other words, if you have had three jobs during that particular year, you will receive three separate W-2s.

Figure: 4 W-2 Statement

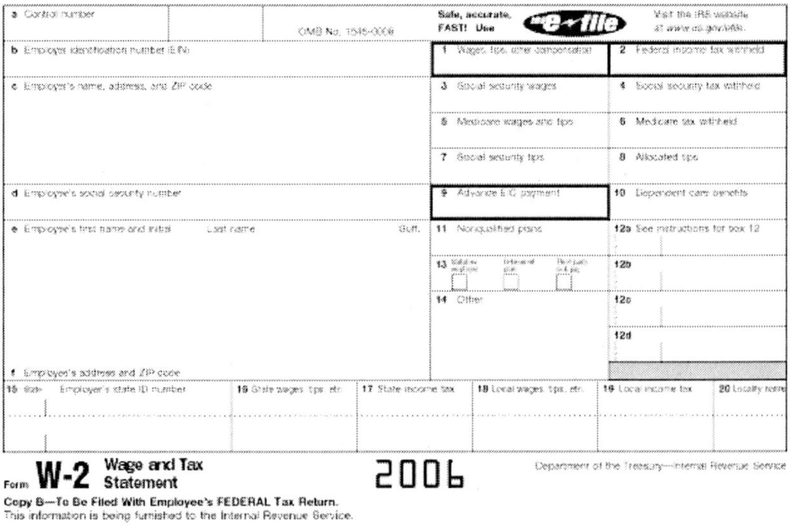
Form W-2 Wage and Tax Statement 2006

Department of the Treasury—Internal Revenue Service

Copy B—To Be Filed With Employee's FEDERAL Tax Return.
This information is being furnished to the Internal Revenue Service.

It is now time to pay your tax! April 15th has arrived and taxes may be due to the federal, state, and/or local government. The information reported on your W-2 is now transferred to your **tax return**. For many adults, this is a very stressful time. It does not have to be so for you. Just knowing the basics such as the due date, which tax form(s) to file, and where to file, can alleviate a lot of unnecessary stress. Check out some basic tax return questions you may have once you receive your W-2.

Frequently Asked Tax Return Questions

When to file?
The IRS (Internal Revenue Service) generally requires that all taxes be submitted by April 15th. If you are unable to file your taxes by April 15th, you should request an extension from your federal, state, and/or local government. If not, you may be subjected to interest and penalties on any outstanding tax liability (amount owed).

What form should I file and where do I retrieve this form?
If you're required to file a federal tax return, you are likely to file a 1040EZ or 1040A form. These forms can be retrieved directly from the IRS by calling 1-800-829-1040 or going on-line to www.irs.gov. State and local tax forms can be retrieved from your state and local government websites. You can also retrieve federal, state and/or local tax forms from your local library or post office.

Where do I get the information to fill in the blank boxes on my tax return?
This information comes directly from your W-2 form(s) and other applicable tax documents received from financial institutions. For example, if you received statements from the bank for interest earned, it generally must be reported on your tax returns. **Important:** There are certified public accountants (CPAs), who offer tax services. Therefore, if you are not sure as to how to complete your tax return, it would be in your best interest to reach out to someone, who specializes in preparing taxes.

Where to file?
You can find out where to file your federal taxes by going to
www.irs.gov. To locate where to file your state and/or local
tax return(s), go to your state and/or local website, and try
linking into the Division of Taxation or Revenue.

Why do I need to file a tax return?
You need to file a tax return to determine if you have overpaid
or underpaid your taxes. If you have overpaid (paid too much)
your taxes, you are entitled to a refund. If you have underpaid
(or not paid enough) your taxes, you should submit a check
with your tax return for the amount of underpayment.

Finally, understand the importance of not trying to avoid
paying your share of taxes. The IRS calls this **tax evasion**.
Tax evasion is when a person attempts to avoid paying taxes
by not reporting all of their income or claiming unallowed
expenses, deductions or dependents on their tax return. As a
taxpayer, it is your obligation to pay the applicable taxes on all
income received. If you try to avoid paying taxes, due to the
government, you will be prosecuted. Remember you can make
huge sums of money, but you must pay taxes, if it applies.

Work Out

Ask your parents to share with you their federal tax returns
from the previous tax year. Spend time reviewing their W-2
form(s), notice how the federal wages in Box 1 agrees with the
amount reported in Box 7 of your parents' tax return (Form
1040). Next, take the other attached supporting documents
(that is, 1099 INT statement listing interest income) and agree
each of these documents to the appropriate lines on the tax
return of your parents.

LESSON 14

Budgeting

"Plan your Work, and Work your Plan"

$\mathcal{A}$ budget is your roadmap to accumulating wealth, and your compass to financial freedom. A budget allows you to control your money, rather than your money controlling you. It is one of the most powerful tools of money management. Sounds awesome, right? Then why aren't more adults budgeting? Some adults do not budget because they believe that a budget is only for Fortune 500 companies. Some others feel that a budget is a straight jacket, conjuring a feeling of confinement. As a result of these misconceptions, many adults are in financial trouble.

Setting up a budget and sticking to it has many advantages:

1. It helps you to live within your means, and not try to "keep up with the Joneses".
2. It shows you where you are spending too much.
3. It helps you to focus on your goals
4. It allows you to plan for unanticipated expenses.
5. It shows you where you have extra money to pay down your debt, save, and invest.
6. It keeps you out of debt.
7. It allows you to apply the elimination process (needs vs. wants).
8. Lastly, a budget allows you to get a good night's sleep.

As you can see, having a budget to live by has many advantages. It is also a necessity if you want to keep your spending under control. So, how difficult is it to develop a budget? It's not. A simple **budget consists of a five-step process**. Let's show you. Grab a sheet of paper and let's get started.

1. First, estimate your total monthly income (like allowance, earned income, and interest), listing them individually, and in the first column. Label this column "Income".
2. Then, estimate your total monthly expenses (like charitable contributions, savings, investments, and lunch money), listing them individually, and in the second column. Label this column "Expenses".
3. Total both columns separately.
4. Compare the income column to the expense column. If they agree, you have a balanced budget. If your income column exceeds your expenses, you need to save or invest the difference. If your expense column exceeds your income, congratulations, you and Congress have something in common, and you need to start trimming the fat. *Just kidding!* You need to review your expenses and determine which expenses can be eliminated. How do you determine which expenses to eliminate? Well, think about it. Did you include more wants than needs? Remember, "wants" are what create debt in many people's lives.
5. Continue the elimination process until you have a balanced budget.

To reinforce the budget concept, take a look at the **college budget example** below:

Phillip is 17 years old and is planning to attend Morehouse College in Atlanta as an out-of-state student. The cost of attending Morehouse College is $30,000 annually. This amount includes tuition, fees, room and board, and the meal plan. Phillip and his parents are uncertain whether they'll have enough funds for Phillip to attend Morehouse. So, as a family, they develop a budget. They begin by writing all the expenses in one column and all the resources (income) in another column. It's important that Phillip and his parents include discretionary expenses (like clothes and telephone) in the budget.

Below is an example of anticipated expenses and resources (income) that Phillip expects to incur at Morehouse College. **Note:** These figures are for illustration purposes only, and do not represent the actual cost of attending Morehouse College.

Phillip's College Annual Budget

Expenses		Resources	
Tuition & Fees (36 credits)	$23,000	Parents' Savings	$13,000
Room & Board	4,000	Phillip's Savings	500
Meal Pan	3,000	Scholarship	5,000
Books & Supplies	2,000	Loan 1(Unsubsidized)	3,000
Telephone	300	Loan 2(Subsidized)	2,500
Auto Expenses	1,300	Work Study	4,000
Entertainment	1,000	Educational IRA	3,000
Clothes	500		
Total	$35,100	Total	$31,000

The difference between the expenses and resources is $4,100. Phillip and his parents should discuss decreasing his discretionary expenses.

- Phillip can save $1,300 by deciding to leave his car at home.
- Does Phillip truly need $1,000 for entertainment, or can this expense be reduced by half ($500)? Phillip has another $500 in savings.

Phillip's expenses have been reduced by an additional $1,800, a difference of $2,300. Phillip and his parents should now consider cutting back on other expenses (like family outings and vacations), or funding the difference with a PLUS loan.

As the above example demonstrates, a budget is not carved in stone. Inevitably, when working with a budget, there will likely be other expenses and income to add or subtract. Therefore, it is essential that you periodically review your budget to determine which expenses can be "pushed around", or determine if there is extra money that you can move into savings or investing. Remember that a budget should give you a feeling of liberation, not a feeling of constriction or confinement, as many adults believe.

Food for Thought
A good budget takes savings "off the top", before paying other expenses.

Work Out

Now, it's your turn! Try developing a personal budget on your own, using the five-step process you've just learned. **Remember:** It must balance.

LESSON 15

Basic Financial Statements

"Financial Report Card"

$\mathcal{H}$ave you heard the saying, "Show me the money". Well, that's what financial statements do. They show you the money. They show you where your money comes from, where it has gone, how much is available, and where it is right now.

Financial statements are also similar to your school's report card. How? Financial statements show your financial circumstances at any point in time. These same statements assist adults and companies in making future financial decisions.

At this point, you're probably wondering, "if financial statements do all of that, why are so many adults drowning in debt"? The reason many adults are drowning in debt is because of a lack of awareness on basic financial statements. And, our school system's failure to incorporate it in the curricula is another cause. As a result, some adults have more liabilities than assets, in other words, owe more than what they own. So, how do you avoid repeating history? Simply by learning how to prepare, and reading basic financial statements.

There are generally two types of Basic Financial Statements:

1. Balance Sheet

2. Income Statement (Profit & Loss Statement)

Balance Sheet

The balance sheet is a snapshot of your financial condition, showing what you own and what you owe at any point in time. **The balance sheet has three categories.**

1. Asset (something you own)
2. Liabilities (someone you owe)
3. Equity (the difference between what you own and owe) or "your net worth".

Assets

Assets are anything owned that has an exchange value. Assets are resources that are expected to benefit you in the future. In addition, assets have the tendency to put money into your pocket. What are some of these assets you can own? Homes, stocks, bonds, mutual funds and, rental property, just to name a few.

Liabilities

Liabilities (debts) are what you owe to others, such as credit card balances and outstanding loans on homes and cars. Unlike assets, liabilities take money out of your pockets.

Equity

Equity is the difference between your assets and liabilities. It is what you are left with after all your debt has been satisfied (net worth). For example, the house that your parents purchased is valued at $330,000, and there is an outstanding loan of $210,000. The difference is $120,000. This difference represents the equity your parents have in their home.

The following equation summarizes a balance sheet:

$$Assets - Liabilities = Equity$$

Income Statement
(sometimes referred to as a Profit and Loss Statement)

An income statement acts like a camcorder. It shows how much money you have made and spent over a specific period. In other words, it shows how much money is coming in, how much money is going out, and how much is left. **The income statement is made up of three parts:**

1. Expenses
2. Income
3. Net Income (or Loss)

Income

What is income? Income is generally money received from different sources, such as employment, interest on savings, and dividends from stocks.

Expenses

What are expenses? Expenses are generally money paid to acquire goods or services.

Net Income (Loss)

The difference between the income and the expenses is Net Income (Loss). If your income exceeds your expenses, you have experienced a profit. You can generally use this profit to make more money. But, if expenses exceed income, you have experienced a loss, and you need to rethink your spending habits. Net income (loss) is sometimes referred to as the "bottom line".

The following equation summarizes an income statement:

$$\text{Income} - \text{Expenses} = \text{Net Income (Loss)}$$

The net income (or loss) becomes part of the balance sheet, which is included in the equity section of the balance sheet.

When you combine both statements, you have a powerful tool to make future financial decisions. As a teenager, it is important for you to understand early in life how to read and prepare basic financial statements. Or, you may have to face the consequences of your mistakes later in life. Unfortunately, many adults are now paying the consequences because they were not taught how to do so while in school. Let's not repeat history. Affirm today that you shall not repeat the financial mistakes of many adults, nor allow your school's oversight prevent you from learning how to prepare and read basic financial statements.

Food for Thought
If you want to become wealthy, learn the vocabulary of money.

Work Out

Now, it's your turn again, try developing a Balance Sheet. Begin by opening a spreadsheet on Excel. Set up two columns with headers, "Assets" on your left and "Liabilities" and "Equity" on your right. Now, list all of your assets (things you own) and all of your liabilities (what you owe). For the purpose of this example, record your personal possessions (like cash, computer, Xbox, and cell phone) as assets. Give each of it some value. This value is its current worth if you were to sell it today. Be sure to include any savings and/or investments you may have among assets. Next, coordinate your debt. Do you owe any family members or friends money? If so, record the amount in the liability column. Total both columns separately. Then, compare the two columns and record the difference in the equity section. If your assets are more than your liabilities, you have equity, and you are in great shape. But, if your liabilities are more than your assets, you are in trouble, and need to exercise restraints. **Note:** The two sides must agree (assets = liabilities + equity).

LESSON 16

Creating a Wealth Plan

"You're in the Driver's Seat"

You have now learned the crucial concepts on how to manage, save and invest your money. Now, it's time to take these same lessons and create a simple wealth plan that will put you on the road to prosperity. Yes, we said simple! About 90% of the first 15 lessons have been incorporated in this simple, seven-step wealth building plan for teens. Check it out!

1. **First, set your financial goal.** This goal can be to save and invest $8,000 by the time you attend college. Next, determine how you will try to meet this goal (that is, through earned income, allowance, and monetary gifts).

2. **Create a budget and stick to it.** Make sure your budget includes needs and limits the number of wants. And, be sure to review your budget biweekly, and adjust it as needed.

3. **Re-familiarize yourself with different types of investments available.** Think in terms of appreciation (stocks and mutual funds) and not depreciation (sneakers).

4. **Adopt the pie chart rule.**
   o Open up a savings account (or certificate of deposit). Deposit your allowance, earned income, gift money and other money, into the bank.
   o When your savings reaches $500, open a mutual fund account with half of your savings.
   o And, when your savings reaches $500 again, invest half of it into a company's stock DRIP plan. But, if you're not feeling "bullish", perhaps "bearish", increase your mutual fund investment, or consider purchasing another investment (like bonds). If you're, though, feeling "bullish", be sure to research the company before investing.

5. **Consider including the 3Ms (money making money) in your wealth plan.** Why not take half of your savings, and invest it into yourself? In other words, a business idea. If you need additional start-up money, give your parents an IOU, meaning, a contract for a loan. Remember that a loan to start a business is considered to be a good debt, assuming that you've done all of your homework. In other words, you've thoroughly researched the business you're looking to start up.

6. **Then, on a monthly basis, create a set of financial statements.** A set of financial statements should include a balance sheet, showing all of your assets (what you own), liabilities (what you owe), and the difference, which is your net worth or equity. Also, develop an income statement, which shows your income, expenses, and net income (loss). Remember, it's important that you know your financial circumstances at any point in time.

7. **Lastly, create an attitude of abundance and know that you deserve to prosper.**

Note: Don't forget to keep your parents involved, as you develop your wealth plan.

Looks pretty simple? So, let's go back to the questions we asked you in Lesson 1, "Why aren't schools teaching students how to manage money?" "Why haven't so many adults learned how to manage their money?" We would love to hear from you.

You can reach us online at: www.blackstreetinvestmentclub.org.

Extra Credit

LESSON 17

Identity Theft

"Safeguarding your most Valuable Asset - YOU"

𝒯oday, we need to be aware of a new type of crime. This crime is called "Identity Theft". Identity theft is one of the fastest growing crimes in the United States and teens are the number one target. What is identity theft? Identity theft is when someone steals your identity to commit criminal activities such as fraud. This person completely takes over your identity before you can use it. One of their goals is to run up thousands of dollars of debt in your name.

So, how would you know if someone has stolen your identity? By learning the warning signs:

1. Discovering that you already have a driver's license when you visit your local Division of Motor Vehicles to apply for a license. And, to add to the confusion, you may have a few ticket violations.
2. Being denied applications for college student loans.
3. Receiving pre-approved bank cards that you did not request.
4. Telemarketers are calling your home and asking to speak with you.
5. Collection agencies are calling or sending you letters of outstanding debt.

As you can see, it is very possible for a perpetrator to completely take over your identity. These perpetrators know that teenagers have clean credit histories and therefore are counting on you and your parents to not periodically check your credit. These same perpetrators also know that teenagers spend hours "hanging out" on the internet. So, what do they do? They lay low and wait for you to sign-on. Then, they begin to "move in" through chat-rooms and pop-up windows. They throw the bait, and you catch it. Next, they convince you, through enticements, to release your most powerful information, your social security number.

Because, teenagers are less educated about identity theft, they are the prime targets. For this reason, teens need to empower themselves by taking **precautions to reduce their chances of becoming a victim of identity theft:**

1. Do not carry your social security card or birth certificate with you. Keep these documents at home!
2. Do not give your cellphone, driver's license, checkbook, or credit card to anyone.
3. Do not store personal information on your MP3, pagers, cell phones, laptop, or other electronic devices.
4. Do not leave your backpack, wallet, or purse unattended.
5. Do not use your mother's maiden name as a password (this is what many parents and grandparents did, and some still do).
6. Do not respond to emails that request for personal or financial information.
7. Do not give your social security number to anyone.
8. Do not share your password with your friends.
9. Do not throw out documents with your social security number on it. Shred them first.

What to do if you feel that someone has stolen your identity:

1. Speak with your parents.
2. Contact your local police.
3. Close any account in your name.
4. Contact one of the below credit agencies and request a credit report
    a. TransUnion @ www.transunion.com or 1-(800) 680-7289
    b. Equifax @ www.equifax.com or 1-(800) 525-6285
    c. Experian @ www.experian.com or 1-(800) 397-3742

REMEMBER: Identity theft can go on for years at your age since you probably have no interest in obtaining credit. Therefore, it is your responsibility to take the necessary action to prevent your chance of being a victim. How do you prevent this from happening to you? You can do so by familiarizing yourself with the warning signs and implementing the above precautionary steps.

Work Out

Speak with your parents about retrieving your credit report with one of the credit agencies mentioned in this lesson. Once you receive your report, review it with your parents to ensure that a perpetrator is not trying to disguise as "yours truly".

LESSON 18

Job Interviewing Techniques

"Be Prepared and Optimistic"

𝒴our application has opened the door, but it is the interview that will get you through the door and into that much sought after job.

In this lesson, you shall learn how to succeed in a job interview. What is a job interview? A job interview is a meeting between an applicant and a representative of a company. The meeting is the result of a job being made available. The purpose of the interview is for the company to get a good look at you, and for you to take a look at the company. So, as you can see, a job interview is a two-way affair. Both parties need to determine if they are well suited for each other.

To simplify this lesson, it has been segmented into two sections:

    1)   General Interview Techniques
    2)   Specific Interview Techniques

<u>**General Interview Techniques**</u>

  1. Resume
     Make sure your resume is free of spelling errors and

grammatical mistakes. Interviewers are often "turned off" to resumes containing errors. Also, remember to bring extra copies of your resume to the interview. You want to be prepared to offer one in case the interviewer forgets or misplaces your resume. This will make a positive impression on your prospective employer and give you a chance to *"show off"* your organizational skills.

Important: NEVER LIE IN YOUR RESUME!

2. **Dress the Part**
   Dress as though you are ready to go to work, and not to a concert. For more information on how to dress properly for an interview, see the section on Specific Interview Techniques.

3. **Remember Names**
   When receiving a letter or a phone call regarding a scheduled interview, always memorize the name of the person, who will conduct the interview. People feel important when you remember and call them by name. This may also work in your favor when it is time for the interviewer to select a candidate for the position.

4. **Be on Time!**
   Always arrive for your appointment 15 minutes early. If you are using public transportation, give yourself plenty of time, just in case you run into traffic. By arriving early, or on time for the interview, you are sending the message that you are very much interested in the job. Also, by arriving early, you are allowing yourself some time to relax before the interview.

5. Don't use Fillers during the Interview

What are fillers? Fillers are words that are not needed to get your point across. Examples of fillers are: "huh", "um", "you know", "like", "ok", "I mean", "like I said", and "but". When you use fillers, interviewers tend to become confused with what is being communicated, and begin to lose interest.

6. Be Polite

Be polite at all times during the interview, and always use the appropriate title (that is, Mr., Mrs., or Miss). Address the interviewer and others by his or her last name. And, only use first names if asked to do so.

At the end of the interview, be sure to thank the interviewer for taking time from their busy schedule to interview you for the available position.

7. Eye Contact

Eye contact is important. Your ability to maintain eye contact tells the interviewer that you are a confident person. Therefore, it is important that you look at your interviewer while speaking and answering questions. Do not look down during the interview. Be focused.

8. Posture

At all times, stand and sit in an upright position. Do not slouch. Guys, drop the "cool walk". Ladies, if you are in a dress or skirt, do not cross your legs while sitting.

9. Be Enthusiastic

The best way you can show an interviewer that you are interested in the job is by smiling, speaking in a confident voice, maintaining eye contact, and asking questions.

10. Cell phone

Turn off your cell phone before entering the room. Do not disrespect the interviewer by letting your cell phone "ring" or "vibrate." When you are in an interview, you are expected to give the interviewer your undivided attention.

11. Reference

Be prepared to submit a minimum of three references to the interviewer. Before you do so, remember to contact your references and get their consent.

12. Write a Thank-You Letter after the Interview

A thank-you letter might just get you the job. Since only a few interviewees take the effort to write a thank-you letter, you may score some additional points. A thank-you letter shows your interest in the job, which distinguishes your candidature, when the final decision is made. Be sure to write and mail the thank-you letter within 24 hours. Do not email this letter. Personalize the thank-you letter by typing it, signing it, and mailing it.

What do you say in a thank-you letter?
- Thank the interviewer for meeting with you.
- Comment on some aspects of the discussion.
- Restate your interest in working with the company.

Specific Interview Techniques

1. **Know the Type of Services or Product(s) that the Company Offers**
Never go on an interview without doing your homework. At a minimum, you are expected to know something about the company you want to associate with. Companies are impressed with candidates who have taken the time to research their background, history, and current position in the industry. Again, this knowledge can help you in winning the job.

2. **Study its Corporate Culture**
Try to get an idea of what the dress code is in the company. You can do this by visiting the company's website or visiting the company before the date of your interview. You want to give the appearance that you can fit in, by dressing accordingly. However, if you are still confused about the culture after going online and/ or visiting the company, it is recommended you wear a suit (tie, if you are a male) if it is an office job. If it is a non-office job, casual dress may be appropriate. What is casual dress? For young men, a pair of khakis, dress shirt, and shoes. For young ladies, a dress (or skirt and blouse), stockings, and low heel shoes.

Below is a list of what NOT to wear to an interview, according to gender.

Females	Males
Heavy make-up	Head bands/du-rags
Large dangling earrings	Multiple wrist bands
Multiple/dangling bracelets	Pants below your waist
Undersized clothing	Oversized clothing
Elaborate hair styles	Disheveled hair
Sandals or flip flops	Sneakers

Both Genders (Male and Females)

- No visible body piercing or tattoos
- No bling-bling jewelry
- No wrinkled clothing

3. **Be Prepared to Talk about Yourself**
   Be prepared to tell the interviewer something about yourself. Share with the interviewer your work experience, education, goals, and reason(s) for choosing the company.

4. **Be Prepared to Answer Questions**
   a. Why do you want to work with our company?
   b. What are your strengths?
   c. Why should I hire you?

5. **Be Prepared to Ask Questions**
   a. What is the company's mission?
   b. Why is the position available?
   c How quickly are you looking to fill this position?
   d. What do you look for in the right candidate?

e. What is the structure of the organization?

f. To whom will this position report to?

g. What type of training program, if any, do you offer?

By asking questions, it shows the prospective employer that you are interested in the job.

6. Close the Sale

How do you close the sale? You close the sale by thanking the interviewer and restating your interest and ability to do the job, and/or willingness to learn. On your way out the door, remember to ask for a business card.

It is important to remember that you are selling yourself to the interviewer. Your goal is to convince the interviewer that you are the only person who can fill the position that is being advertised. To do so, you must be able to handle the interview successfully. How? By familiarizing yourself with the interview techniques you just read.

Work Out

Based on the interviewing techniques you have now learned, perform a role-play game with your parent or another adult. As the interviewee, you have applied for a job and now have to land that job. To do so, you need to implement the techniques you have learned in this lesson. Continue the role-playing game until you "Ace It".

LESSON 19

Peer Pressure and Staying Positive

"If You Want to be an Eagle, Stay Away from the Turkeys"

*W*hat is Peer Pressure? Peer pressure is the influence that people of similar age or status place on others to encourage them to make certain decisions or behave in certain ways. There are two types of Peer Pressure – Positive Peer Pressure and Negative Peer Pressure.

Positive Peer Pressure

Positive peer pressure occurs when your peers use encouraging words and other behaviors to inspire you to "do the right thing". When you get the support of your "real friends", you can make tough decisions and not give into negative peer pressure. These friends encourage you to stay away from those who drink, smoke, abuse drugs and join anti-social elements. These friends encourage you to join a school committee, study for a test, or engage in productive activities.

Negative Peer Pressure

Negative peer pressure occurs when your peers try to get you to do something that you "know is wrong". These "so-called friends" might try to convince you that it is cool to use or sell drugs, drink alcohol, smoke cigarettes, *"cut class"*, and disrespect your parents or other adults. You may do so, because you want your "so-called friends" to think you too are cool. Remember, there is nothing cool about doing something unsafe, illegal, or something that goes against your family values. When you allow others to convince you to do something that you "know is wrong", it only shows your inability to make the right decision, and your lack of leadership skills. The best way to handle these "so called friends" is to *"dis them"*.

Here are some ways to handle negative peer pressure:

   a. Have friends with similar family values.
   b. Avoid situations that might get you into trouble.
   c. Respond with "talk to the hand".
   d. Pay attention to your own feelings and beliefs.
   e. Choose to be a leader and not a follower.
   f. Build on your self-confidence.
   g. Choose your friends wisely. Do not choose friends who smoke cigarettes, use drugs, cut classes, join gangs, or lie to their parents.
   h. Talk to someone you trust when you are under pressure.
   i. Say a definite "**NO**" and walk away.
   j. "Stay positive".

<u>Staying Positive</u>

Staying positive requires on-going work. Staying positive also demands that you "Keep it Real". "Keeping it Real" means having confidence in yourself, being happy with who you are, and not allowing others to define you. It means staying "above" the influence and not "under" the influence.

So, how do you stay positive when you are stressing about the test next week? How do you stay positive when you are having disagreements with your siblings and parents? How do you stay positive when you live in a neighborhood with "gang-banging" and drugs *"running rampant"* throughout your neighborhood? And, how do you stay positive when you are being pressured to have sex?

You stay positive by:

- Spending time with your family
- Spending time with friends who have similar values and beliefs
- Participating in physical activities, not street gangs
- Believing in the existence of a higher being
- Maintaining a positive attitude
- Being responsible
- Making good decisions
- Being a positive role model to other teens
- Doing volunteer work
- Valuing your education and setting goals for the future
- Maintaining a healthy diet and getting enough rest
- Talking to your parents or someone close, when you feel stress

As a teenager, you are bound to experience positive and negative peer pressures. It is your responsibility to learn how to handle the influence of negative peer pressure before the situation gets out of control.

Work Out

Identify two additional ways by which you can continue to maintain a positive state of mind/attitude. Then, implement a written plan that will allow you to incorporate these positive ideas/attitudes into your daily life.

LESSON 20

Self-Made Millionaires

vs.

"Just-Getting-By" Mentality

"Do You Want the Pie or the Crumbles?"

*W*hy are some people destined to be rich, and others are destined to be poor? Why do some people sail through life and others struggle to pay for even the basic needs? How is it that two people set out from the same "starting line", everything being equal, and one person overtakes the other? What do self-made millionaires do differently from people, who are "Just-Getting-By"? The answer to all of these questions is simple: They think and do things differently.

Unlike many others, self-made millionaires do not have a "just-getting-by" mentality. Self-made millionaires know that they are the architects of their lives, and that there are no limitations as to what they can do in life. They expect to be successful in life, and commit to do whatever it takes to ensure their success. They understand that anything is achievable in life with hard work.

Check out some of the characteristics or qualities of a self-made millionaire:

a) Task-oriented
b) Disciplined
c) Focused
d) Persistent and
e) Think big

So, how do you avoid the "Just-Getting-By" mentality? You can do so by studying the thoughts and actions of self-made millionaires as oppose to "Just-Getting-By" people.

Self-Made Millionaires	"Just-Getting-By" People
Hang out with winners	Hang out with losers
Risk taker	Play it safe
Strategize	No plan
Excellent performers	Poor performers
Play the money game as an offense	Play the money game as a defense
Excellent receivers	Poor receivers
Play in the big league	Play in the small league
Travel outside of their comfort zone	Stay within their comfort zone
Play the game to win	Play the game to "just-get-by"
Take great leaps	Take small steps
Seize opportunities	Run from opportunities
Set goals	Lack goals
Allow the mind to focus	Allow the mind to wander
Focus on all the reasons "you can"	Focus on all the reasons "you can't"
Looking to hand out	Looking for hand outs

Thoughts are powerful! Your thoughts will determine how successful you will be in life. How? Because your thoughts will direct the actions you take in life. So, be careful about what thoughts you allow into your mind. If you tell yourself you can't, you won't. If you tell yourself you can, you will. Self-made millionaires tell themselves they can, and they do.

Food for Thought
Change your thoughts today, so that you may begin living an abundant life tomorrow.

Work Out

Everyday, set aside some time from watching television and talking on your cell phone, and review the keys of self-made millionaires. Then, watch how quickly your thoughts shift in the same direction.

LESSON 21

Giving Back

"To Whom Much is Given, Much is Expected"

*I*n Lesson 8, we shared with you how your money may be divided with the help of a "Pie Chart Rule." We fractioned one part of the pie for "giving", and we used church offering as an example. However, this is not your only choice. There are many charitable organizations for which you can donate money and/or your time. For instance, if you enjoy caring for animals or want to help the homeless, you can go on-line to learn more about the different charitable organizations that provide services for abused animals or homeless people. Visit www.Guidestar.com. Or, if you wish to participate in a walkathon to promote cancer or aids awareness, contact your local cancer or aids awareness group to learn more about what they do, and how you can make a difference.

Once you find a charitable organization, how do you ensure that your monetary donation is being spent for the mission? With the help of your parents, contact the charitable organization and inquire about how much of your donation will be contributed to supporting the cause, and how much will be used for administrative expenses. If you are fine with the allocation, give your parents your donation, and ask them to send a check, on your behalf, to the organization.

Other ways to "give back" that are not monetary:

1. Donate clothes. All teenagers feel good when they look good. So why not participate in a clothing drive. Remember to ensure that the donated clothes are in good condition.
2. Since most teenagers want to belong to the "in crowd", you might want to reach out to those who feel left out and invite them into your circle.
3. Are you a student who does not study hard but yet ace every test, quiz, or project? If so, why not offer to tutor one of your peers who is not as excellent as you at academics.

Remember, when you take the time to help someone, you make a positive impact on the life of that person as well as yours.

Work Out

Look around your community to see what you and your friends can do to improve it. Put it in writing and share it with your parents and friends. **Then, take action!**

Wishing you a Bright and Prosperou$ Future!

𝐵*lack* $*treet Investment Club* (SM) (Teen Club)
www.blackstreetinvestmentclub.org

About the Author

Ms. Sheryl Ridley Dorsey is a Certified Public Accountant with over 20 years of experience. She also has a Masters Degree in accounting with special focus on taxation from Rutgers University. She currently has a practice in Burlington County, New Jersey. Ms. Dorsey holds CPA licenses in the states of New Jersey and Pennsylvania. She provides tax consulting, auditing, and accounting services to individuals as well as businesses.

Ms. Dorsey is concerned that the average student who graduates from high school lacks basic skills in the management of personal financial affairs. She observes, with dismay, that most school curricula forget to include subjects like money management, and that many parents and grandparents fail to set a good precedent on financial responsibility. Impelled by her avid interest in education and the urgent need to address financial illiteracy among teenagers, she founded the Black $treet Investment Club, Inc. (B$IC) in September 2000. Every third Wednesday, she teams up with its 17 motivated teen members to engross in fun learning sessions on money management.

"MONEY MANAGEMENT FOR TEEN$" is a compilation of her fruitful interactions with the members of the B$IC over the past seven years. Written in a simple and engaging style, the book breaks down complex principles of earning, saving, investing, and spending. If you aim to better understand and apply the best practices in money management, you are holding the right book. If you wish to secure your financial future and lead a more productive and fulfilling life, read on!

About the Contributors

ROMAINE BARNES is a 16-year old, 10th grade student. He has been a member of the investment club since 2002. His favorite subject is Math, and he enjoys playing soccer. His favorite basketball team is the Lakers and favorite football team is the Eagles. Romaine plans to attend college and study Electrical Engineering.

RAMONE BARNES is a 16-year old, 10th grade student. He has been a member of the investment club since 2002. His favorite subjects are English and Art. Ramone plans to attend college and study Architecture. One of his goals in life is to be wealthy.

JORDAN DORSEY is a 13-year old, 8th grade student. He has been a member of the investment club since its inception. His favorite subject is History. He enjoys playing basketball and football. His favorite basketball team is the Sixers and favorite football team is the Eagles. He has an interest in playing college football and plans to attend college. Jordan favorite quote is "Just Do It" (Nike).

RICHARD FLETCHER is a 14-year old, 9th grade student. He has been a member of the investment club since its inception. His favorite subjects are Language and Science. Ricky enjoys playing basketball. His favorite basketball team is the Sixers and favorite football team is the Eagles. He plans to attend college and study Psychology, and play basketball. Ricky favorite quote is "Keep on Keeping on".

BERNARD FOWLER is an 11-year old, 5th grade student. He has been a member with the club since 2005. His favorite subject is Math. He enjoys playing football and baseball. His favorite football team is the Falcons. He plans to attend college. Bernard favorite quote is "Get Active".

CALEB HENRY is a 15-year old, 10th grade student. He has been a member with the club since 2004. His favorite subject is Math and Science. He enjoys track. Caleb plans to attend college.

COLLIN HILL is an 11-year old, 5th grade student. He has been a member with the club since 2005. His favorite subjects are Math, Science, and History. He enjoys playing football and basketball. His favorite football team is the Kansas City Chiefs and his favorite basketball team is the Nuggets. He plans to attend college and study History. Collin favorite speech is "I Have a Dream", by Dr. Martin L. King, Jr.

LOGAN HILL is an 11-year old, 5th grade student. He has been a member with the club since 2005. His favorite subjects are Math and History. He enjoys playing football and basketball. His favorite football team is the Steelers and his favorite basketball team is the Cavalier. He plans to attend college and study History. Logan favorite speech is "I Have a Dream", by Dr. Martin L. King, Jr.

BRANDON JOHNSON is a 15-year old, 10th grade student. He has been a member with the club since 2005. His best subject is Math (Algebra). He enjoys playing basketball and his favorite basketball players are Tracy McGrady and Dwyane Wade. He plans to attend college and study Engineer. Brandon favorite quote is "If You Fail to Prepare, be Prepared to Fail".

KENNETH JOHNSON is an 11-year old, 7th grade student. He has been a member with the club since 2005. His best subject is Math. He enjoys playing basketball. His favorite basketball team is the Rockets. He plans to attend college and join the NBA. Kenneth favorite quote is "Let's Go!"

RYAN LUMPKIN is an 11-year old, 6th grade student. He has been a member with the club since 2005. Ryan best subject is Math. Ryan enjoys playing basketball. His favorite basketball team is the Sixers. Ryan plans to attend college and play professional basketball.

KURT PHILIPS is a 15-year old, 10th grade student. He has been a member with the club since 2000. His favorite subject is Chemistry, English, and History. He enjoys playing football, basketball, and running track. His favorite football team is the Falcons and his favorite basketball team is the Timberwolves. Kurt plans to attend college and study Engineering

MARCUS PHILLIPS is an 11-year old, 6th grade student. He has been a member with the club since 2000. His favorite subject is Science and Math. He enjoys playing football and running track. His favorite football team is the St. Louis Rams and his favorite basketball team is the Miami Heat. Marcus plans to attend college.

BRANDON ROGERS is a 13-year old, 8th grade student. He has been a member with the club since its inception. His favorite subject is Math. His favorite basketball team is the Sixers. Brandon plans to attend college.

ANDREW STEWART is a 14-year old, 8th grade student. He has been a member with the club since 2003. His favorite subject is Math. He enjoys playing basketball and his favorite team is the Miami Heat. He is good at selling and handling money. He plans to attend college to study Business Management. Andrew plans to start his own business.

SHERARD THORNHILL is a 13-year old, 8th grade student. He has been a member with the club since its inception. Sherard best subject is Math. His favorite sport is football, and favorite team is the Eagles. He spends much of his spare time working with his father at his business. He understands the meaning of hard work. Sherard plans to be an entrepreneur.

MONEY MANAGEMENT
FOR
TEENS
ORDER FORM

Methods of Ordering

Fax Orders: (609) 267-5334   Send this form.

Postal Order: Black $treet Investment Club, Inc.
                          6 Turnbridge Drive
                          Lumberton, NJ 08048
                               or
                          P. O. Box 302
                          Lumberton, NJ 08048

Website Order: www.blackstreetinvestmentclub.org

Please send book(s) to:

_____
Name

_____
Address

_____
City   State   Zip

_____
(H) Telephone

_____
(W) Telephone

Cost: $13.00 x _____ copies = _____
Taxes: 7%   = _____
Shipping & Handling Charge $4.60 per book x __ = _____

Total Cost: = _____

Please make check payable to Black $treet Investment Club, Inc.